End On A Win

Robynne Mirau

"Give, and it will be given to you, good measure, pressed down, shaken together, running over, they will pour into your lap. For whatever measure you deal out to others, it will be dealt to you in return."

Luke 6:38 NASB

Dedication

Coach Todd Clark, Coach Bob Newstrom,
Coach Nathan Radzak

And the 2001-2002 Marshall Varsity Basketball Team

Pete Newstrom	Luke Mirau	Geoff Udjur
Dan Baumgartner	Aaron Sillanpa	Pete Lien
Justin Nelson	Ian Kramer	Gustav Brandstrom
Adam Machones	Duncan Mapes	John Sterle
Mark Stauduhar	Charlie Lenz	David Owo

A truly amazing group of men
Thank you for all the support and love you gave

and to

Dr. John Fetter
For being more than a physician, for becoming our
friend

****

Written for:
Our children
Luke, Amanda, and Abigail
Always remember the lessons of faith, love, and
laughter

3

Special thanks to...

Teresa Peterson, Karen Newstrom,
Sara Floerke, and Abigail Mirau

Contents

Foreword

In the spring of 1998, I walked into Marshall School to apply for the position of Head Coach of the boys' basketball team. The first person I saw there was Greg Mirau. I knew him from the junior high basketball circuit in the years previous, both as an opposing coach and also as a referee.

While I did not recall his name from the brief pre-game introductions we had seasons before, I vividly remember one over-riding thought: "I hope this man is the Athletic Director." If this gentleman, with whom I'd had only positive experiences, was doing the hiring, I might have a chance landing this job. Unfortunately, upon our re-introduction, he informed me that he was not the A.D. However, very fortunately, I was hired as the coach and my first priority was to ask Greg if he would be my assistant coach. He accepted.

From that point on, we went to work attempting to build a quality basketball program. We were lucky to work with great kids from day one; however, the players' hard work and good attitudes did not result in winning records the first few seasons. Our first three years coaching together resulted in records of 6-18, 5-18, and 10-14. Lack of wins can cause parents to complain about the head coach, and also the head coach to question himself. This is where Coach Mirau kept things positive and moving in the right direction. He never wavered in his support of what I was trying to do – he always had my back. He would (and still does to this day) tell the players how lucky they are to have me for a coach, how hard I'm trying and if they continue to listen to their coaches, they'll be alright. I'm not sure if I always believe it, or if the players do, but I know that *he* does. That's a tremendous asset to have when it seems that everyone else is a critic.

Greg and I were challenged and rewarded in our fourth season – the reason for this book. It was as if his stubborn

9

support and love for the team had finally been realized. With his son, Luke, as a senior, and with Coach Mirau and his family struggling to overcome one medical emergency after another, our basketball team made it to our first state tournament ever. His contribution didn't, and still does not, end there. Our team went 24-4 and 20-8 the following two seasons and we hope to be good again next year (no matter when you are reading this). We appreciate the great support we enjoy now, but when I reflect back to the building years, my main source of support was never in question: Greg Mirau.

Today I feel that basketball was just something that has put us together. Greg is the most kind and generous man I have ever been around. I know of no one who has a negative thing to say about him, and if they did, I would dispute it. In addition, to his strong investment to the Marshall basketball program, Greg has been a great source of comfort and friendship in my personal life. In January of 2000, my wife, Misty, and I lost our first child to miscarriage 9 weeks into the pregnancy. I went to Marshall to tell the team what happened and that I would be gone for a while. I thought I was holding up fine; trying to be strong for my wife. I saw Greg in his office first and as I told him, I began crying. He held me in his big bear hug for what seemed like an hour and I just kept on crying. Instead of feeling strange or ashamed, I felt safe. To know you are with someone who cares for you and whom you can trust is one of the best feelings in life. Sometimes, I wonder if any other head coaches around have an assistant like Mirau...they should be so lucky.

In closing, I will give you the two pieces of advice Greg often gives our team: "Listen to your coaches" and "Love is a great motivator."

Todd Clark
Head Coach Marshall Boys Basketball 1998-2011

Spring 1956

In a small northeastern Minnesota town, a young mother takes her three young children to the doctor. The older two have been fighting colds and congestion and it seems time to have the doctor take a look. In the office that day, the doctor carefully listened to the chests of the two older children, making a diagnosis as necessary. Just because the little guy is with his Mom and brother and sister, the doctor takes a listen to his chest too.

Coincidence? Maybe. But probably actually providential. What the doctor heard in that random check became a life-saving moment for that little guy. Something did not sound right with his heart. The recommendation? Get him to the University Hospital and let the doctors look at him.

So a trip to Minneapolis and the University Hospital was made. It was a four-hour trip and some anxious times for the parents. The diagnosis made? The little boy had a pinched aorta and surgery would be needed.

That little guy was my husband, Greg. In 1956 he had major heart surgery to repair the pinched aorta. A scar runs from the front of his chest around to his back. That successful surgery repaired the aorta. His mother says the surgery was performed on a Monday, and by Friday he was running in the yard of the hospital. That surgery was probably about the 200th done by a leading pioneer surgeon, Dr. Lillehei, who is considered the father of heart surgery.

He must have done a good job because Greg went on to play all the sports he wanted, leading a full and active life, having all the blood flow he needed.

CHAPTER ONE

YOU NEVER KNOW WHAT A DAY WILL BRING

"Be strong, and let your heart take courage.
All you who hope in the Lord." Psalms 31:24 NASB

Winter 2002 – January 10

"I know God is hearing our prayers and taking care of us, I just don't feel like it is doing any good. Daddy keeps getting worse instead of better."

This is a quote from Abbey, our then 14-year-old daughter, several days into the toughest ordeal of our family's life. We knew the Lord; we knew where to find the answers; we had a terrific support team around us. A ton of people were praying, and still the days dragged on and on. Would there ever be an end? In January of 2002, our lives were changed forever.

Greg and our three children were at school, a normal day with the normal routines. Greg is a physical education and health teacher at the Marshall School in Duluth. MN. He also has coached boys' basketball on various levels for many years. The past few years, he had served as the assistant varsity basketball coach working closely with head coach Todd Clark. Because all three of our children attended Marshall, each morning they would travel with their dad. In the afternoons, during the basketball season, I would pick up the girls from school, head home, prepare supper, and wait for the "boys" to come home. That Thursday, January 10th, was like any other day.

One of the things Greg does each morning when he gets to school is to stand in the hall near the entrance and greet the kids as they come. Kids he doesn't even teach look for him there each day for the warm smile or high five. It is kind of known as his post, right there outside the gymnasium doors.

His connection to the school has grown over the 10 years he has taught there and he has developed many terrific friendships with both the staff and students. I'm amazed at how many past graduates of the school come back to get a hug, update him on their lives, or stay connected by e-mail. Greg just knows how to love people.

Greg Mirau really is a people person, though a bit on the shy side. He never draws attention to himself but sits back and watches others, contributing when he has something to say. But his heart is so big and pours out so much love that people are drawn to him. They come to him for counsel, for prayer, for a hug, for the latest joke he might have, or just to have someone make them smile.

At a recent school reunion one of Greg's co-workers came up to me and thanked me for letting so many hug Greg and for sharing him with others. I learned early in our marriage that that would be a part of our lives--sharing Greg.

We have three children. Luke, our son, was 18 and a senior in high school that year. He loves school, basketball, and being with his friends. Luke is a reserved kind of kid with that same quiet spirit, yet strong sense of humor, like his dad. His dad is his hero, his coach, his friend, his mentor, just about everything to Luke. They understand each other and communicate well. They have always had a great bond and nothing has ever threatened it. A big part of that bond has been their love for basketball. Greg had been able to be Luke's coach for most of Luke's basketball years. That extra time together formed an even closer connection between father and son.

Amanda, our daughter, was 16 and a junior in high school that year. I call her the second wife sometimes because she is so perceptive and supportive. She and her father are best friends. She seeks his counsel on many issues. She knows and loves that he is fiercely protective of her – every boy on campus knows it too! Amanda has a strong relationship with God and has always been able to see His hand on life. She is a joy to have around, but even this experience challenged every aspect of her life.

Our youngest Abbey, then 14, is outgoing, fun loving, a kind of free spirit type of girl. She was a typical 8th grader where everything is very serious and nothing is too serious. Abbey had to do some major growing up that year and that was tough. She, too, is very close to her dad and our incredible journey forced her to face some real fears.

While I was at the school that sunny January day, Greg came out to the car to say hello before he headed back in to work. He was scheduled to referee a couple of basketball games that afternoon before he headed for the varsity basketball practice. He bid the girls and I goodbye and told us he would see us in a little while. He had worked out on the treadmill that day and told me that a former student had been by and that they had shared a good visit.

Greg is always doing extra jobs to make money and that day he was refereeing basketball games for the younger teams. I was making a favorite dinner of his and waiting for their arrival when the phone rang. It was Greg and he said, "Hi, Honey, I'm not feeling well. I have some chest pain so I'm going down to the hospital to get it checked out. I don't think it's anything, but Gorby thinks I should get it checked out. I should be home in a little while."

Gorby, Chris Gobeck, is the sports trainer for the Marshall School and he is always there for games and practices, taping ankles, icing sprains, and doing whatever is needed to be done. Greg sounded fine and had no sense of worry in his voice; I decided I would not worry either. After all, it didn't sound too serious. I hung up the phone and then I immediately began to wonder. As we live about a 25 minute drive outside of town, I decided to call our friends Scott and Pam Anderson, who live in town, and see if they could meet him at the hospital and let me know if anything was discovered. Even though they were in the middle of their dinner, they agreed to do so. This saved me a trip to town, and I didn't have to alarm the girls if there was no need.

I continued with dinner preparations, slowing everything down since I realized the guys would be late. Pam called back in about an hour saying they were at the hospital and Greg was resting comfortably. They didn't know anything yet. She would call me again after they ran some more tests and finished checking out Greg's condition. It was comforting to know someone was there monitoring the situation for me. I relaxed a little. The second phone call came and it was not anything I expected to hear. She said, "You need to come to the hospital now. They are going to do surgery on Greg. I'll explain when you get here."

I hung up the phone totally bewildered. What was going on? I gathered the girls and told them Daddy needed some surgery and we were going to the hospital. I asked them to pack some items to be able to stay overnight. Luke came home after basketball practice; having been told his dad was taken to the emergency room. Greg had asked Gorby to speak with Luke after practice, letting him know what was up with his dad and telling him to head home with the car. After some discussion it was decided he would stay at home and take care of the dog. I promised that I would call him later as soon as I knew more.

Luke had just turned 18 and probably had never stayed home alone overnight. Someone was always around. Now all of a sudden, and at a crisis point, Luke took on that responsibility. He handled many, many phone calls that night.

I remember getting some things together and beginning to pray. You know how it is when your head is just spinning and you have no idea why? Well, that's what mine was doing. On one level I didn't seem to be feeling anything; on the other I had this uncanny calm inside of me that allowed me to be responsible and take charge. I quickly called my sister, Barb, Greg's mother, Evelyn, and some friends to let them know briefly what was happening.

I gave Luke a hug, told him I loved him, and the girls and I hopped in the van and headed for town. On the way I prayed, "God, let me be planted on the Rock. Let my faith be steady on a firm foundation. I want and need to flesh out my faith, no matter what we are going to be facing." I didn't know till many days later how important that prayer would be.

I had made arrangements with our friends, Kim and Lu Chart, to leave my van parked at Kim's dental office, right across the street from the hospital; a "perk" Kim let me use when I needed to visit someone at the hospital. They assured me they would be praying.

As the girls and I arrived at the hospital, Pam was there to let us in. She directed us downstairs to the emergency room where Greg was. We quickly rushed in and found Greg looking fine and resting comfortably. There was already a group of people there, visiting with Greg and everyone seemed relaxed. They were monitoring Greg's blood pressure and heart rhythm, but not much else seemed to be happening. One by one the girls and I leaned over to hug Greg. He assured us he was feeling fine; he was not in any pain. To be honest, Greg looked great, not at all sick or uncomfortable. I remember an internal sense of relief that he was probably just fine.

After a few minutes, Dr. John Fetter arrived back in Greg's unit. We were introduced and he shook my hand warmly. Dr. John Fetter was the heart surgeon on call that night. I don't suppose either of us knew what an incredible journey we were beginning.

CHAPTER TWO

THE DOCTOR ON DUTY

"...He who prepared us for this very purpose is God."
II Corinthians 5:5 NASB

January 10

Although he was a complete stranger to me, I was immediately at ease with Dr. Fetter. I felt a genuine kindness in him and realized that our lives were in his hands. He directed me over to the side of the room and placed the x-rays up on the lighted chart for me to see the damaged aorta. With incredible "smarts" he explained in detail what had occurred and showed me the torn aorta. Greg would need immediate surgery. The heart team had been called and they were waiting for them to arrive. Dr. Fetter explained what the surgery would involve, how he would fix the damaged aorta and possibly replace the aortic valve, if it seemed necessary. An ultra-sound machine was brought in, and the technician zoned in on the aorta. Within a moment or two we were all looking at the screen, watching in amazement as the tear in the aorta flapped with each beat of Greg's heart. It is a picture that will never be totally erased from my mind. It was so unbelievable to watch that flapping tear.

Dr. Fetter was great to point out the details of the picture and help us understand, as best we could, what we were seeing and what would need to be done to repair the injury. Greg asked if the surgery could be done in the morning. I think he was hoping his family could go home and sleep and come back in the morning. Dr. Fetter looked at Greg and asked him, "Do you want to die?" There was no time to waste.

Being a health teacher, Greg was very interested in what was happening and wanted to explain in detail what he knew to me. I remember that I didn't want to know so much; it was all so overwhelming. Surgery was needed; let's get it done, but don't involve me with all this information. I kind of brushed off his detailing of the scenario. I think at that point I was concentrating on just staying upright.

Also in the emergency room that night was my family practitioner. I had only had one appointment with her since our regular doctor had retired. I did not know Dr. Lisa Prusak very well, but it was good support to have her there. Since we had not secured a family doctor yet, Greg asked her if she would be his doctor, she agreed. Dr. Prusak became a comforting face and support to us through this journey, and I really felt her offer a genuine friendship.

I was keeping an eye on our daughters, wondering what was going on in their minds. The tears were flowing, but I also saw them being brave. How frightening it was for them to see their dad lying there, to realize he was headed for surgery. Their whole world had taken a major blow and been turned upside down in a matter of minutes. They love their dad so much and are very, very close to him. To see them express that love and offer comfort and prayer support to their dad was amazing to watch. Of course he was loving them back.

What is so incredible at this point is to learn what a torn aorta means. Generally if someone's aorta tears, they might take five steps, and then fall over and die. Since Greg's situation, many people have told me stories of men they know who have died suddenly in similar conditions. Greg heard a pop in his chest, felt constriction, was sweating and had pain. Even so, he ran the length of the court one more time (remember, he was refereeing a game), and then called a time out and pulled himself from the game. He told Mr. Schoer, his partner that night, that he needed to take a break, that he wasn't feeling well. Mr. Schoer (Terry) thought maybe Greg had the flu or something. He waited with the teams for a few minutes and then headed out of the gym to see what was wrong. In the meantime Greg found Nathan Radzak, another coach, to take his place as a referee and found a reffing shirt for Nathan to wear. Terry and Nathan headed back to the gym to finish the game, neither knowing what was happening with their friend Greg, but not having any real concern. Having taken care of his immediate responsibilities, Greg then had the trainer Gorby look him over in the back room.

Gorby has been the sports trainer at the Marshall School for many years. He loves his job and enjoys the challenge of getting injured athletes up and running as soon as possible. Gorby told me that Greg looked very white, that his symptoms were narrowing vision and that his chest hurt. He took Greg's pulse and said that it would be fast and then slow. He asked Greg briefly about his history and if there had been any other symptoms, which there had not been.

Greg was thirsty and Gorby got him some water, which seemed to make Greg feel better. Gorby's initial thought was that Greg was having a heart attack or a stroke. Either way, he felt Greg should head for the hospital. They discussed calling an ambulance, but opted to have someone drive him down. After all, Greg was beginning to feel a lot better. Gorby found Bob Newstrom, another assistant coach, and asked him to take Greg down the hill to the hospital. Gorby told Greg it might not be anything, but if it was, they would know what to do. Gorby asked Greg about calling his wife, and in a few minutes Greg did so. He told Gorby later, "You don't know how hard that was to call my wife." Gorby assured Greg he would be down to the hospital in a few minutes. Still on his own strength, Greg walked out to Bob's car.

Bob Newstrom told me that as they headed for the hospital they prayed together, from the beginning committing this whole journey to the Lord.

When they arrived at the hospital Greg walked himself in to the emergency room. Already Greg had defied the odds of survival. When he told emergency that he was having chest pain they immediately put him in a wheelchair and began to give him a blood thinner. The first assumption is that he was having a heart attack.

They did an immediate chest x-ray and a CAT scan. It didn't take very long for them to pull the blood thinner. It was clear Greg was bleeding inside.

After speaking to Coach Clark and Luke, Gorby headed for the hospital. He was able to spend some good moments with Greg in the emergency room, getting the report on what was wrong. He told me later that he knew of Greg's great faith and assured Greg in the emergency unit, "The Big Guy upstairs is watching over you. There is nothing to worry about." Greg nodded in understanding.

Dr. Fetter commented to them both that he was glad they came to the hospital. Because Greg had begun to feel better, he was considering just going home. Dr. Fetter told him, "If you had headed home, you would have died." Greg looked at Gorby and thanked him for being there and for directing him to the hospital. Gorby played an instrumental part in saving Greg's life that night.

Another interesting point is that Dr. Fetter was at the 2nd half of the basketball game Greg had been refereeing that night to watch his own son play. While he was there, his pager went off and he headed for the hospital. He met Greg and asked him what he was doing and what happened when his symptoms began. Greg told him he was refereeing a game at Marshall. It is amazing that these men were both at the same game, only in different periods. God had everyone, everything we needed in place that night. Dr. Fetter told Greg he had been at that game watching his son; he hadn't seen Greg there. Greg told him he had pulled himself out of the game because of how he was feeling. These men probably had passed each other on the road, one heading away from the hospital, the other heading toward the hospital, not knowing that in a few minutes their lives would be strongly linked together.

Dr. Fetter assured me in the emergency unit that because Greg was young and strong, he had a very good chance of surviving the surgery. Already God had given Greg the grace and fortitude to endure that long; he was, after all, bleeding inside. Generally an aorta tears crossways and the patient bleeds to death quickly. Greg's aorta had torn the length of the aorta where an aneurysm had formed. There are three layers of tissue to the aorta and Greg's tear was on the inside layer. Thus he had "extra time" because although he was bleeding, the outer layers of tissue were containing it, for the moment at least. Dr. Fetter told us later that it was interesting to watch the blood pooling and swirling inside the aorta before he began the surgery. Already we had received so much grace.

I called Luke from the hospital and filled him in on what would be happening with his dad and assured him I would call in the morning. I asked him if he was okay by himself and was he doing alright. He told me he was busy receiving calls from people who had heard his dad was sick. Luke tried hard and did a good job informing people of his dad's situation.

The emergency room nurse sought me out to tell me I had a phone call. I could not imagine who would call, who really even knew we were there. It was our friend Kevin Nordstrom. I had asked Luke to call him and let him know that Greg was having surgery. I knew he would be praying for us, but Kevin wanted to do more. He said he was on his way to the hospital. Kevin is a single parent and I knew it would not be easy for him to come. I also knew that by now his little girls were already tucked in bed. I assured him he did not need to come, but to stay with his girls. He told me everything was covered and he would be there shortly. Kevin's presence that night was a great support and comfort to me. Kevin works in a hospital and on a daily basis sees a lot of different things. He offered a lot of insight to me that night and did a great job of just "being there." Already, without even trying or asking, I had a nice support team at the hospital.

Inside the emergency cubicle where Greg was, Abbey stood by her dad's side. It was their moment alone. She pulled out of her backpack her baby blanket. Since she was very little, she has always "shared" her blanket with her dad when he took a nap. On a lazy Sunday afternoon when her dad was snoozing, she would creep quietly into his room and cover him with her own blanket. It was a moving sign of compassion from her that she thought to bring it to him that night. He told her he would use it when he got his own room. I felt tears coming watching that moment, seeing how much my daughter thought to love her dad that night.

The heart team arrived and someone announced they were ready to go. Greg would be wheeled away from us. As he left we assured him of our love and prayers. I said to my husband, "I release you to the Lord if He wants you." He told me, "I've released myself." I gave him a kiss, told him I loved him, and they rolled him away.

It's a poignant moment, that incredible separation time when you realize you may never connect that way again. I had every reason to hope. But in my heart I knew that it was possible I would not see Greg again, this side of heaven. It felt as if time stood still for a moment and I remember feeling a shiver go through me. My mind wondered how much our lives were going to change.

CHAPTER THREE

WAITING A LIFETIME

*"Therefore do not be anxious for tomorrow; for tomorrow will care
for itself. Each day has enough trouble of its own."*
Matthew 6:34 NASB

January 10-11

Karen Snyder, principal from the Marshall School arrived
at the hospital. Pam Anderson, our friend we had called to
initially go to the hospital to be with Greg, had called Karen's
home, and her husband, Kevin, had tried to reach Karen by
cell phone to direct her to the hospital. She was working late
that night at school. As soon as she was home, her husband
sent her on her way to the hospital. While driving she called
the school administrator, Marlene David, and the high school
principal, Chris Johnson. It meant a lot to me that Greg's
place of employment and those peers showed up. They
carried with them the full support and prayers of the school.

Karen first saw Greg in the emergency room and was
amazed to see him sitting somewhat upright and visiting. She
sensed and saw in Greg a real confidence about the situation
and she told me I seemed so calm and strong. Didn't we
know this was open-heart surgery? I told her later that I
probably seemed calm because I had to transition so quickly
from "shock to no choice." I really didn't have time to stir and
worry. The girls were teary and scared so she knew we had a
good dose of reality and did know what was coming.

While she was with Greg in the emergency unit, Greg in
his usual manner was trying to take care of things. He told
Karen his grades were on the computer and asked if Nathan
Radzak could be his sub. Nathan was in need of employment

27

and Greg was anxious to help him have a job. He then wanted to know if there was anything else the school needed from him. She was amazed but not surprised. Greg is just very responsible.

Our small group now growing, headed for the surgery waiting room on the 4th floor. I was familiar with this room having waited there with some of my own family members when they or their spouses had needed procedures done. I knew where to go. It was a little too familiar. We walked that hallway, most of us in some level of disbelief.

So quickly the course of our lives had changed. The plans that we had for that evening were not to be realized. Instead, destiny had placed before us a new schedule, one we had no choice in. I think about that amazing moment, when everything changed, and all the emotional adjustments needed to be made in a matter of minutes. On that walk down the hall to the waiting room, all of us, on some level, were trying to make those adjustments.

Chris Johnson met us in the 4th floor waiting room and soon behind him Greg's sister, Florence, and her friend, Rod, arrived. Greg's mom had called them, and since Flo lives in town she zipped on over. I don't know that I could have thought to call her. I was glad that Greg's mom had.

Scott and Pam Anderson were still there. Before long John and Thomas Parr showed up, coming all the way from south Superior. Greg has coached and taught both of these guys. I was overwhelmed that these two young men would come so far, late at night, just to be supportive. John told me later, "When we got the call about Mr. Mirau, Thomas and I just looked at each other and said, 'Let's go!' It wasn't an option. We didn't know what we could do, but we knew we had to go." I could see a real fear in them but also a strength to give to our family. I embraced them both and tried to find strength in myself to give to them. At this point I could not give them any answers but I tried to offer positive statements to them. Mr. Mirau would be back.

Kevin Nordstrom arrived soon after. He had actually been on the 7th floor trying to find us and was waiting there. Someone asked him who he was waiting for and they directed him down to the 4th floor. Scott and Meg Lucas, more friends of ours, showed up next. I was so surprised to see them. Luke had called them and it wasn't an option in their minds but to come right to the hospital. You learn something in these times about the relationships you have built over the years and how the blessings come back to you. Here, without any effort on my part, was my support group. Some I knew well, some I hardly knew. It was going to be a long night. We settled into a corner of the room that seemed to offer comfort. My back was to the wall and I could see the door of the waiting room if anyone should come in.

The Parr boys left after a while, and I wished them a good night's sleep. Scott Anderson asked his wife Pam if she was staying the night. She nodded yes to him. I asked him to please take Amanda and Abbey to his house to get some rest. Although they didn't want to go, I felt it was best. Who knew what was coming? They would handle it better on some sleep than on none. I assured them we would call first thing in the morning. I know they struggled to leave and probably really wanted to stay close to their dad and I. I knew Scott would give them good care, and I prayed they would fall asleep. Scott taking them that night was huge for me as I could just focus on Greg and allow God to take care of the kids. None of us really knew what we were facing.

At about 10:30 pm, a surgery assistant came out from the surgical unit and gave me Greg's wedding ring. It fit perfectly on my pointer finger. Flo, Greg's sister, came over to touch and hold it for a minute and then gave it back. She just needed a connection to her brother. We began to wait.

It was about 11:00 pm when the surgery began. They told us they would come out occasionally with updates and to call into surgery whenever we wanted. For some reason I had no need to call in there. Flo did a few times. It made her feel better to get updates.

The conversation was solemn and quiet. Some people shared about members of their own families and the surgeries they had faced. Flo reminisced about her and Greg's dad's surgery and spending time in that same waiting room. Chris Johnson shared a bit about his own father's surgery. Many were success stories.

Because they had work the next day, Karen and Chris headed to their homes offering me their home and cell phone numbers and insisted that I call if either could do anything for our family. I thanked them for coming, and we chatted briefly about a statement to be made to the school the next morning. After all, Mr. Mirau would not be in his classroom.

I remember commenting to Pam how unreal this was and wondering how this could be happening. We were all in shock that this perfectly healthy man was now facing life-threatening surgery. We learned later that this procedure is the most difficult surgery done in Duluth. I'm glad I didn't know that at the time. I remember Dr. Fetter really assuring me that he knew what he was doing. He had done a similar procedure not too long ago and Greg's youth was on our side. He had an 80% chance of survival. Good odds.

Scott Lucas is a professional psychologist and I knew he was watching me, seeing how I was doing. He commented to me saying, "Robynne, I don't know how you are doing, but I am really wrestling with God. This may be God's time to take him, but I'm telling God not now. I am not ready to let Greg go. I am really wrestling with God."

Silently, Kevin was wrestling on the same level. He knew how huge and risky this surgery was and was extremely worried; however, he hid that from me and just sat by me being supportive.

The group gathered in our room got to know each other as the night wore on, each making connections about how they knew Greg, what their relationship to him was, etc. It's amazing how quiet a hospital can seem in the night. We were the only ones in the waiting room, and aside from some maintenance workers and night shift people, the hospital seemed very still.

Inside of the operating room, it was not so still. As the staff assembled to do their jobs amazing connections began. Two of the operating room nurses were cousins of a friend of Greg's and mine. The anesthesiologist, Paul Anderson, was also a friend. When he got the call to come to work for surgery, he had no idea he would be working on a friend. There was a surprised look when he saw Greg lying there.

A special bonding time took place that evening. I'm not sure that people really understand what they can give to each other, or what we receive from other people. Life becomes so chaotic at times. Sometimes we are too busy living to pay much attention to life. A bond developed inside of the operating room, and a bond was also forming in the waiting room. People working and waiting together all focused on the same person, were hoping for the same goal of a successful operation.

In a nearby operating room another friend was performing surgery. He told Greg later that all he heard in OR was, "we have a train wreck coming in, we don't think he'll survive." He did not know till three days later that the "train wreck" was his friend, Greg.

It is interesting that the statement made by the staff in the operating room that night shared very little hope, but our statements from Dr. Fetter gave us every reason to feel confident. I never really felt that I would not see my husband in the morning. I had no sense or fear of his death.

You do try to prepare yourself that death is a possibility. The mind works to help the emotions handle two completely different outcomes. It really does "boggle the mind" when the thought processes take on two journeys at once. That is what mine seemed to be doing. I was trying to prepare myself inside of my head for all the possibilities, even though I had no idea what they really were. All I really knew was that we just had to get through the night. It would be a long time until morning light, but I had hopes in the sunrise of tomorrow.

Occasionally Florence would call into the operating room and get an update. Mostly they just said he was stable and that the surgery was going okay. I began to feel glad that no one was coming in to see us from the operating room. I think I believed they would only bring bad news at that point of the night. Scott and Meg Lucas now took off with a promise to be in touch and to keep us in their prayers.

By 3:00 am some of my support people were getting tired. I couldn't blame them; none of us had come rested and ready to go. Pam and I decided to take a walk and stretch our muscles. Sitting there for hours was really getting to me and some fresh air sounded good. We headed out to the skywalk and walked back and forth taking in the city from above the street. It was quiet and mostly still outside with only a little traffic moving. The night looked beautiful with the moon and stars shining. Was anything in the world any different? At that moment, it didn't seem like it was. It became almost a momentary escape from the horrible reality that was thrust upon our lives just hours before. Pam patiently listened to my ramblings, trying to comprehend what was happening along with me.

We decided we should head back to the waiting room. I didn't want to be gone too long. Unfortunately we didn't realize as we left the hospital for the skywalk that we were now locked out of the hospital. As we stood by the sliding door trying to figure out how we would get back in, a gentleman came off the elevator. We knocked on the door and he let us in. Thank goodness or we would have been running the streets without jackets looking for the way back in. It became a humorous moment in the midst of the heavy stuff we were feeling.

There was no way I could sleep and Kevin felt the same way. As Flo, Rod, and Pam rested, Kevin and I continued quiet conversations. The clock moved slowly forward, the moments carefully ticking by. Dr. Fetter said the operation could take from a few hours to thirteen. I was ready to give him all the time he needed.

In my mind I would try to imagine what the scene inside the operating room was like. I would picture staff and doctors surrounding Greg, all carrying out their duties and responsibilities. Then my mind would picture Greg, lying on the operating table and my imagining would stop. I did not want to see his face lying there. Many times that night my mind would take that journey and then stop. It was just too painful to believe that Greg was inside the surgical unit and that all those people were working on my husband.

A real sense of peace stayed with me for most of the night. Even in my fatigue, I felt clear headed and closely guarded by the prayers of people. I look back now and realize how gracious God was to give me such a peace. I wasn't panicking; I really wasn't afraid. I just felt shock and peace. I'm grateful for that good beginning. I would need it in the days ahead.

At about 4:00 am the surgery assistant came out to tell us that the surgery was completed and that all of Greg's vitals were strong. Greg had survived the surgery! They were working on containing some bleeding and when he was

33

completed, the doctor would be out. I thanked him for the update and the waiting continued. It would be another three hours before we would see Dr. Fetter's face.

At 7:00 am Dr. Fetter joined us in the waiting room looking tired but quietly confident. The surgery was successful, the aorta was repaired. He had replaced the aortic valve and Greg was resting in recovery. He had some concerns about bleeding but was hopeful that they had been able to stop all the bleeders. I remember him keeping an "open door" that they might have to go back in, but he was hopeful that it was contained.

He encouraged and directed us to head up to the Intensive Care Unit on the 7th floor. As soon as they had settled Greg, I could see him. We gathered our few belongings and moved upstairs. Pam and Flo made phone calls for me to let people know that Greg had survived the surgery. Kevin, relieved that Greg had survived the night, left to go to work. He told me he would see me at lunchtime. I hugged him goodbye and thanked him for being there. Unlike me, he still had a full day of work ahead of him.

I called Luke at home and let him know his dad had come through the surgery okay and was now resting. Luke told me of the people he had talked with the previous night. He had handled a lot of phone calls but was doing okay. He decided he would go to school that day and then come to the hospital later. He had not had much rest, but he needed and wanted to stay on schedule. I don't think the idea of spending hours at the hospital appealed to Luke on any level. I don't blame him. On his own, Luke found his own balance of life and trauma and how to handle both.

Scott A. brought the girls back to the hospital to me and around 9:30 am, after I had seen Greg, we headed home to get some rest. As far as we knew, Greg was stable and what he needed most was rest. On the way home, I answered the girls' questions as best as I could. I really didn't have many answers. I was still trying to figure out what had happened.

We arrived home to the answering machine blinking. As we pressed the button for the messages, we never envisioned it would be Dr. Fetter. But it was. Greg was still bleeding internally and they were headed back to surgery to try to find the bleeder. I remember him apologizing in his message, but there was no choice. I looked at the girls and said, "We need to go back."

CHAPTER FOUR

MORE WEIGHT, MORE WAIT

"He heals the brokenhearted, and binds up their wounds."
Psalms 147:3 NASB

January 11

The girls and I changed clothes and freshened up. I called our neighbor, Teresa Peterson, to tell her we were heading back to the hospital. Would they check on the dog and let her out for us? Immediately and without hesitation, Teresa said she would be right over to take us to the hospital and that Brad, her husband, would see to Mini, our dog.

She was at our home in a matter of minutes and drove us back to the hospital, concerned that I hadn't had any rest. Her caring for us in that moment became a pattern that would be repeated many times over in the coming weeks. I am sure I could have driven the 20 miles into town again, but how nice to be cared for in that moment. I was exhausted from the long night and it was safest for me not to be driving.

So many people came and became the strength for our family. They would do what was needed, carry the prayer load, run the errands, provide food, send money, and embrace and hold my kids. As I look back on our journey and remember those who stepped up and made the contacts with people and communities who needed to be reached, who ran the errands, who cared for the children and I, I know I understand the "body of Christ" better than at any other point of my life. Others became the eyes, the ears, the legs to help as we "ran that race" before us.

We returned to the hospital and checked in at the waiting room. I was directed to a smaller room that was filled with people. I was stunned to see so many there! It amazed me that by 10:30 or 11:00 am the next morning so many people had heard of Greg's crisis. Our former Youth For Christ director, Larry Williams, and his wife, Gail, were there. I couldn't imagine how they even knew. It was an awesome thing that so many people had heard of our ordeal before 24 hours had elapsed. The little room became an armful of hugs and love for the girls and I. Our prayer and emotional support group was growing.

I looked around the room at each and every one of them, so grateful and so overwhelmed and so tired. But here they were, all willing to be there for us. Laurie West and her husband, Craig, were there and had brought a tray of food. What a comforting thing for them to do; the girls and I had not had time to eat. It wasn't that I was hungry, (you really don't think about eating in crisis) but I knew that we had to take care of ourselves too. Many people would remind me of that.

Because the waiting room was so full, Teresa decided to go find her brother, Dr. Patrick Twomey, who also worked at the hospital. It so happens he is a pathologist so she headed toward his department. Her brother Pat was quite surprised to see his sister and asked her what she was doing at the hospital. She explained about Greg being her neighbor and briefly what had happened. He asked her what his full name was and then took her over to where he was working. At that time, Dr. Twomey was examining Greg's aorta, and he showed it to Teresa. How amazing! Teresa likes to tease Greg that she has seen his aorta, and even Greg has not! Her brother examining the tear in that damaged aorta was amazed to hear that its owner was still alive.

Each person who came seemed to have a reason they needed and wanted to be there. As Dr. Fetter came into that small waiting room, he struggled to find my face among the crowd. Approaching me, he assured me that they had found the bleeder and were able to stop it. Greg had received some more blood, and everything seemed stable. Again I was grateful. He told me he was heading home for rest but that the hospital knew to call if there were any changes. Even though I had not slept in 24 hours, I knew I would not be heading home.

There were so many people around and so much information to think about and process. As we headed back up to the ICU waiting room, I was able to pause and hug individuals. I thanked them for their presence and support, answering as best I could their questions and giving assurance that I believed Greg would now be fine. I received a call from Marlene David from the Marshall School and was able to give her the most recent update. Always in the back of my mind was keeping the school informed. I was concerned how the student body was doing. As we left that room to again go up to ICU, Gorby, the trainer from Marshall, was there in the hall. I hugged him and thanked him for sending Greg to the hospital. His counsel had literally saved Greg's life. Gorby was just glad that things had worked out well and assured me he was praying for us.

In the meantime the school had prepared a statement for the student body at Marshall to receive that morning. The announcement stated, "Mr. Mirau, Marshall health and physical education teacher and basketball coach, underwent heart surgery last night. Skilled physicians and nurses are caring for him at this time and he appears to be doing well. Mr. Mirau and his family would appreciate your good thoughts and prayers but have asked that only family visit the hospital right now. We will put large 'get well' posters in the middle school and upper school offices during the lunch hour so you can write him a short message, if you would like."

Chris Olds, a sophomore that year and a basketball player, said, "I remember that I was watching the seventh grade boys basketball game the day that Mr. Mirau had his heart complications. I left just before the eighth grade game started, which I heard was when he had to go to the hospital. The next morning, I was sitting in French class when someone brought in a note for Madame Firling to read. She told us that Mr. Mirau had been sent to the hospital. Adam, Dave and I all looked at each other with surprised looks. We talked about how we had all seen him just the afternoon before." I knew I was feeling shocked; I wondered how much more the team and students were feeling it.

I did not allow the girls to go see their dad that morning. I felt it would be too shocking; he wasn't awake and I wanted to protect their minds from those scary images. I don't think they appreciated me at that moment, but I found I was faced with decisions that I could only answer on instinct. In the afternoon when Luke arrived, he went in to see his dad. Although he was brave, it was still shocking for Luke. He pulled together all his strength and put on a brave face, but I knew his heart was breaking. He told me he was glad the girls had not been in there yet and did not think I should let them see Dad.

Teresa had gone home to take care of her family, but assured me she would be back to pick the girls and I up. Our youth pastor, Brandon, stopped by and took the girls to Youth Group that night. Luke headed up to school for basketball practice and I had time to sit with Greg and not be focused on my kids. Greg had been through two surgeries already. He lay there resting, the ventilator assisting his breathing, the many machines monitoring his vitals, and nurses coming in and out continually assessing him. I stood by his side, stroking his swollen hands, praying silently for God's mercy for my husband. Tears slowly worked their way out of my tired body. How unbelievable the scenario before me was. I stood their alone, exhausted, afraid, and stunned.

It was late in the day but not quite 24 hours since Greg had entered the hospital and I was in the waiting room visiting with a number of people when the nurse summoned me to please come into the ICU. I went directly and was immediately introduced to a neurologist. Greg was experiencing some weakness in his left leg and they were concerned that he may be experiencing a slight stroke. They would ask Greg to push with his leg against their hand and it was obvious that the left leg was not as strong as the right. I remember the weight of a thousand bricks falling on my shoulders at that moment. The tears welled up in my eyes and I fought with every bit of strength I could find to be brave. The doctor was not convinced that it was a stroke. He just wasn't sure. He wanted to wait a bit before running any tests. Greg's left foot had a strong pulse and was warm to the touch. The circulation seemed to be fine, there was just a little weakness when they asked him to push against their hand. They assured me they would monitor him closely and, if needed, run tests for a possible stroke.

I walked out of that ICU unit feeling that I could not survive any more bad news. The weight of it all was threatening to knock me to the floor. How could God allow a stroke to come after all we had been through? Had Greg not suffered enough? What would I tell the kids? How would we survive? I was so tired, running on empty already, and now I had a new burden to bear.

CHAPTER FIVE

GOOD AND BAD

"My grace is sufficient for you, for power is perfected in weakness."
II Corinthians 12:9 NASB

January 12

For the first 24 hours of Greg's hospitalization, I didn't know where the checkbook was or if we had any cash. It had been such a hard day and I was discouraged by the unnerving thoughts of a stroke. I knew I needed to tend to my children and stay strong for them. Teresa had brought us home and fed us, or maybe more correctly, made us eat.

When Luke came home from practice that evening, he had gifts of bread and food and a card signed by some of Greg's co-workers. Another card was there with my name on it and inside was a $100 in cash, a gift from another teacher. Someone had the foresight to meet our needs before I could even begin to think about them. Both vehicles were in need of gas, and we didn't have to scramble or rush to find Greg's wallet or checkbook. The needs were being taken care of.

We crawled into bed totally exhausted. I prayed fervently that Greg's weakness would not be a stroke and pleaded with God to please heal my husband.

Amanda had made some calls to her friends that evening, seeking prayer and friendship support. She had taken our bedroom phone to her room that night not thinking anything of it. She fell asleep with it in her room. We were all so tired, and although I felt I couldn't sleep, sleep came.

I was startled in the night by the phone ringing. I jumped out of bed fumbling for my phone, which wasn't there. By the time I reached another part of the house for another phone, it was done ringing. No message left. Amanda was so tired, she never heard the phone ringing in her own room.

We called the hospital that morning and they told us Greg was stable and that the doctor would meet with us when we arrived. Dr. Fetter met me at the hospital and told me he had tried to call in the night. I explained to him how I could not find my phone. During the night Greg continued to point to his leg and complain of pain. When the nurses lifted the sheet covering his leg and looked they were shocked to see it swelled to about three times its normal size. Greg had suffered vascular collapse in the left leg. When the blood was reintroduced to his system, one vein collapsed and would not allow the blood to flow. Although some blood movement was happening, enough to give his foot warmth and a pulse, much was pooling in the leg causing the leg to "balloon" to accommodate the increasing blood. This increased pressure was compressing the muscles and nerves in that leg.

Immediate surgery was needed and done to relieve the pressure Greg's leg was experiencing. I don't even know the name of the doctor who did the surgery in the night, although I think someone had told me. The surgery involves making two incisions on either side of the leg to relieve the pressure and allow the muscles breathing room, a procedure called a fasciotomy. When I saw Greg that morning his leg was huge, bandaged and elevated. The enormity of the leg with its wrapping just drew my eyes. What had happened? It was unbelievably huge.

The nurses told me this condition is called "compartment syndrome". It occurs occasionally in athletes whose muscles are used a lot and are strong. When they no longer have the pressure of blood keeping them expanded, they can collapse and are not able to re-open. This is what had happened to Greg and what had caused his weakness. Many asked me if they should not have seen this coming or happening. Was it the hospital's fault? I don't know but I don't think so. All of the prescribed procedures for post-coronary care were being done. The compartment syndrome was a rare combination in relation to heart surgery.

Dr. Fetter said he had only seen the syndrome in relation to heart surgery once before. Thankfully Greg was able and alert enough, and in enough pain, to point to the leg and get the nurses to look at it. Because he was still on a ventilator, there was no way he could speak to them. In many ways, he saved his own life. If the compartment syndrome had not been caught when it was, it could have taken Greg's leg, or even his life.

So we now had more weight added to our burdened hearts. I remember sitting in the waiting room a little later and being so overwhelmed by all that had happened in such a short amount of time. Greg had gone from being perfectly healthy, at least as far as we knew, to being in the hospital in ICU. The disbelief is incredible. The heart and soul cannot possibly process everything quickly enough to support the emotions. A numbing sensation just takes over, I suppose to help one survive. Some would call it shock. I did have the presence of mind to feel some relief that Greg had not had a stroke. Good news, bad news.

Dr. Fetter came and sat with me for a few moments in the waiting room. He assured me that everything with Greg and the aorta looked great. His numbers, blood pressure, etc. were doing fine. He felt confident about the initial surgery. He did say to me, however, that the medical battle now was Greg's leg. They had caught the leg in time to save it, but it would have to be watched carefully for infections or complications. I told him I just couldn't believe all that had happened to us, and I felt the tears welling inside. He squeezed my hand in understanding.

He stood to leave, paused, turned around, and said to me, "Robynne, I know you're a person of prayer. We are all praying. We've done what we could. Greg is in the Lord's hands now." He turned and walked away. I could see in his shoulders the burden God had placed on his heart for my husband and our family. I knew he carried our situation with him as he went on to care for other patients.

You see, as a teacher in a private school, a lot of the students Greg has in the classroom have parents who are doctors. John Fetter was one of those people. Before our journey was done, it would be a band of doctors with kids who had Mr. Mirau for a teacher. Not only were there normal expectations of the doctors to do their medical best; but they also had the added pressure of accounting to their kids at their supper tables at night. I remember one of the doctors specifically telling me that. The added support of students who were very concerned for their teacher became an added blessing for us.

So now Greg had three doctors on the case: our heart surgeon, our new family physician, and now a leg doctor. Dr. Ken Kaylor became Greg's primary leg doctor. He would oversee the future care of the leg.

All of his doctors would swing by on a regular basis, but many other physicians who were friends or parents of students at the Marshall school were beginning to stop in ICU. In fact, Greg began to have so many medical staff visitors that the nurse told me Greg was a popular guy. Dr. Fetter said he was more popular than the mayor!

The revolving door on Greg's room became so busy that they finally posted a notice on his room that stated, "Only immediate family and the following doctors allowed". They then listed the doctors on the case. One physician friend told me later that he stopped by to see Greg and they would not let him in. Greg's nurse Julie told me later she was the one to throw him out. It wasn't because they didn't embrace the support of people, Greg just could not get any good rest with continual company. To be honest, I didn't realize how many doctors Greg and I really knew, but it was quite a lot, especially those who knew Greg.

Julie came to me later and said, "No wonder he's such a popular guy. He is the kindest man I've ever taken care of. Even when I do things that hurt him, he thanks me." I think she had already developed a special tenderness to Greg and our family, but I am confident she treats all patients with the same gentle care. Julie does a wonderful job in a highly technical nursing position in post-coronary care. She has the medical qualifications and also a wonderful bedside manner. I appreciated her many times over.

CHAPTER SIX

PERSPECTIVE IS EVERYTHING

"Bear one another's burdens, and thus fulfill the law of Christ."
Galatians 6:2 NASB

January 12

On Saturday morning I had a few minutes to myself in that now way too familiar waiting room. I sat back contemplating all that was going on. Praying, thinking, praying, hoping, praying, fearing, back and forth my mind went. I felt so lost as to how I could, or should, help Greg. While I had not yet fully understood the initial surgery we had faced, I was now trying to digest information on this third surgery for his leg. In the first 24 hours of Greg's hospitalization he had been through three surgeries. This is on the same man who three nights ago was playing basketball with his son at the school.

It is hard to understand compartment syndrome fully. I asked our leg specialist, Dr. Kaylor, at one of our post-hospital appointments, if he could give me a brochure or a flyer of information on this condition. He looked at me, and said, "No." There apparently is not much written on the subject because it is so rare.

In relation to a heart surgery, they had only seen it happen once before. How unique is Greg? They did tell me that because his leg was so swollen they would have to do several surgeries, called "wash-outs" of the leg to clean out any dead tissue. Then they would look for signs of infection and watch the muscles to see if they had survived the pressure they had been under from the syndrome. Since his initial leg surgery occurred in the middle of the night on Friday, his first "wash-out" would be on Sunday morning.

They told me the doctor on call that weekend would do the surgery.

On that first Saturday, shortly after my meeting with Dr. Fetter, the family began to arrive. For the most part, I had not seen any of my family since our initial entrance to the hospital. It was pretty emotional for me to have my brothers arrive with their wives and families. My parents had both passed away years before. So far I had been with friends and neighbors. But now it was family, a lot of family who I knew had been praying for and thinking of Greg and me and the children.

I took the girls in to see their dad that morning. They could not stand to wait any longer and I felt they needed the connection, the visual to see their dad still here. I prepared them as best I could, telling them he could not speak to them and that he had a lot of monitors, but he was doing good. They were brave, strong girls and put on a smiling face for Dad. They visited with him and encouraged him. We read scripture and prayed. They had questions about their dad's swollen hands, the ventilator, and so on. I did my best to help them understand everything that was happening. If you have never been in an Intensive Care Unit, it's a difficult place to understand and comprehend. After we left him to rest, they both cried. It is just so hard to see someone you love all wired up. Fortunately for me, out in the waiting room there was family to lean on, and they did.

One of the visits that really impacted me was from my brother Dan. He had been through several angioplasties and finally a heart by-pass surgery to correct a chronic plugged artery. I spent many days at that same hospital with him. It was easy for me to be there for him as I live in Duluth and I had time to spend. I remember watching how difficult it was for him and his family to face all those times of uncertainty.

But they had finally achieved a successful operation and he has been doing well.

Having him come and knowing how deeply he understood our journey brought tears to my face. The first thing he said after an initial hug was, "Come on. Let's take a walk." He took me away from the waiting room, the barrage of people, the heaviness of the moment and just talked to me. He assured me that what I was facing was far more difficult than what Greg was facing. He talked to me about what it is like to be on the inside, everybody taking care of you, the doctors and nurses hovering over you, machines monitoring all the vitals of your body. He knew that the really painful time was for those on the outside facing the uncertainty and bearing the weight of the moment.

We walked to the other end of the hospital, a long slow walk and stood by a window and talked. I don't suppose he knows how much strength he gave to me in that walk, but it was a lot. Having deep conversations about life isn't something we do on a regular basis, but it was neat to know that we could. It helped me to express to my brother my disbelief of what was happening to Greg. I expressed a lot of fears, but he assured me Greg was strong and a fighter. I think he also told me Greg was too ornery to die. A little humor brings a lot of healing.

We headed back to the waiting room and my waiting family. I think back now and realize it was good for me to walk away from the people, the situation and take a break. He was really the first person to get me to leave the area during the day. It was a positive step for me. He helped me find a little different perspective.

My sister, Barb, came that day as well as my brothers Clyde, David, and Gary with their wives. I hugged and embraced them all. Is there anything like family in a time of crisis? It pulls you back to your roots, to your childhood when you all grew up in the same house. A connectedness reoccurs, and you know the foundation you have to stand on. I am grateful for a wonderful, solid family.

One of the Marshall families, John and Toby Sillanpa, whose son, Aaron, plays basketball, called me at the hospital to say they were preparing supper and would deliver it to the waiting room. I assured them they didn't need to do that, but what a blessing when she delivered a meal, big enough to feed my whole family. God was surely meeting every need.

My brothers Dave and Gary really honed in on my daughters. Abbey volunteers at the zoo where Dave is a zookeeper, so they have a special bond. I knew she would talk with him. Gary is the kind that likes to indulge people at the moment, and he found ways to treat the girls with food and fun. They took them downstairs to the hospital cafeteria for ice cream treats and helped to distract their fears. The girls love their uncles so much.

The waiting room was filled on a continual basis with our friends and family. I would be visiting with someone and look up to see new people coming. Our neighbors, Mark and Brenda Toms, showed up that day. I was moved as I went to embrace them and thank them for coming. Brenda was in tears, crying for Greg and our family. Such compassionate moments really touched me. I updated them as best I could and assured them that for the moment, Greg was stable.

My brothers went in to see Greg, assuring him they were there and wishing him a speedy recovery. They would squeeze his hand and speak with humor and love, telling Greg he was going to great lengths to get attention. He nodded in agreement, knowing he was being teased.

Later in the day I brought my sister Barb in to see Greg. She had come prepared to stay with us having taken the week off from work. I explained to her about Greg's new mechanical valve. She asked Greg if he could hear the clicking and he nodded yes, and then snapped his fingers to the beat he was hearing. With so many machines in the room monitoring Greg, we really could not hear the valve. Now we hear it on a regular basis!

Coach Clark came by also that day and I brought him in to greet Greg. He gave Greg an update on the team and practice and told him not to worry about a thing, just get well and come back to the team. Coach Clark is a shy guy in his own way, but he has a great respect for Greg and they made a good team coaching together, both learning from one another. I appreciated Coach that day, bringing strength to Greg, and encouraging Greg to keep on fighting. I knew Coach would bring back a positive report to the team.

CHAPTER SEVEN

TEAM TRIALS

*"Anxiety in the heart of a man weighs it down,
but a good word makes it glad." Proverbs 12:25* NASB

January 12

The Marshall Basketball team had already begun that season to work on their bonding. They were sharing meals together after Saturday practices. We had cooked for and fed the team in our home early in the season. It was fun to see and share in the connectedness that was happening, on and off the court, between the team members and each one with their coaches.

The first two evenings of Greg's illness the team did not hold official practices. Instead they met and prayed for their ill coach. Coach Clark told me when he first heard of Greg's illness that there was immediate doubt -- could Greg really be that ill? But then the next immediate was concern. This team cared about each other so much. Coach Clark had stopped by ICU that first evening, checking on what was happening and immediately offering support and prayers. He told me that whatever I needed or the kids needed, just ask. He had no expectations for Luke to be at practice or games. He wanted Luke to have the freedom he needed to deal with his dad's illness. Not far behind that statement was the full support of the assistant coaches and the team.

Saturday evening brought the first basketball game for the team since Greg's illness began. I spoke to Greg saying I thought I should go attend the game. I told him I wanted to support Luke and the rest of the struggling team. He nodded in agreement. Friends offered to stay with Greg so some of the family and I headed to the Marshall School, just up the hill from the hospital.

It was a difficult decision to know what was the right thing to do. Do you stay by your critically ill husband or do you try to help the kids maintain some type of normal life? No one had handed me a manual on crisis management. I was on my own with many decisions. Amanda was a manager for the basketball team and Luke played. I went with my instinct to believe that continuing life was important for the kids. Coach Clark had no expectations for our kids at this point, they could do whatever they needed. I encouraged Luke to be at the game and to play and assured him I would be there. He promised his dad he would be back with the score after the game. Again, Greg nodded his approval of our decisions.

Re-entering the gymnasium where Greg's aorta had torn was so difficult; I was grateful to have family by my side. I felt anxious facing the Marshall basketball community and all the people who knew what had happened. Would they wonder how I could be there, why I would leave Greg? I was concerned about their opinions of me being there and not at the hospital. I did not need to be as floods of hugs and well wishes came that night and continued at each game I attended. Being parents, they knew I was there for Luke. I also think my being there gave them a sense of hope that maybe, just maybe, Coach Mirau was going to be alright.

Aaron Sillanpa's grandmother is a great fan of basketball, her grandson and the team. That night, and each game after, it became her pattern to hug and kiss the girls and I. Her loving, mothering embraces are still given to us today. It was so nice to have that "grandma" loving us like that.

One man who really reached my heart that night was Dr. Todd Freeman. He is a friend of Greg's and his son, T.J., was under Greg's coaching in the past. He came over, put his arm around me squeezing strongly and said, "You hang in there

Robynne. If Greg survived the first night and that surgery he is strong and he will survive the rest. You hold on to that." I did hold on to that statement many times in the coming weeks. Todd gave me a vote of confidence in that statement, and although it made me cry, I will never forget that moment or his words. Again, it re-adjusted my perspective. I was feeling anxious about the issues in front of me that day. Todd helped me see how much Greg had already survived.

Luke played poorly that night, but Coach Clark let him play a lot, trying to help him think about something other than his dad. I wondered what was going on inside the mind of Luke and the rest of the team. This was the first game for them where Coach Mirau wasn't talking to them on the floor, or patting their heads when they got back to the bench, or talking some defensive strategy. Many of these boys had had Greg for a coach for five or six years. Dan B. and Pete N. both told me it was very hard to focus on the game knowing how ill Coach Mirau was. The team had always taken a moment of silence before the games, but now it became a moment for prayer, Dan leading the team before each game, asking that they would play their best and asking for God to heal their coach.

I had asked Pam to pick up little message cards of hope and trust in God that I could give the team to encourage them and remind them that Greg was thinking of them. She picked out two possibilities and when Coach Clark came by that afternoon, I let him select the one he thought best. He passed them out to the boys before the game that night. Many of the guys told me later they read them a lot and kept them in their wallets. I wanted them to have something to hold onto from us. I wanted them to know we were thinking of them as they were thinking of us. They are a fabulous group of young men, but what a major weight to carry with them each time they entered the gym. Pete Newstrom told me that in many ways

Dan's praying took the role that Coach Mirau had always brought, the role of the spiritual encourager. For the entire team a member of the family was missing. For many of the team members, Greg was the dad and in that role brought a lot of leadership. They knew how strong Greg's faith was and they put their own out there, too, for their coach.

For Geoff Ujdur, a junior on the team, there was even more burden. Besides hurting for his ill coach, he was carrying additional weight. Around Christmas time one of his best friends was in a car accident. He had immediately headed to the hospital. He said, "I think I reacted that way because ever since my father died of cancer when I was six years old, I have always had the greatest fear of people close to me dying." He had visited at the hospital with his friend before heading for the game at the Esko holiday tournament.

His friend's girlfriend had also been seriously injured in the accident so he wrote their initials on his basketball shoes, just for support to both of his friends. He ended up tearing his ACL (knee ligament) in that game and his season playing basketball was over. He remembers that Coach Mirau was the one to come to him and give medical attention. It was the first time in Geoff's life to be that seriously injured. In that 24-hour period, he had a lot to carry. The Wednesday before our journey began, Coach Clark's son became seriously ill, which made the whole team sad, and the next day Coach Mirau was in the hospital.

Geoff says, "I remember being in the small gym and having a team huddle and hearing for the first time what had happened to Coach Mirau. It was complete shock."

Later that night at home, I had my first chance to really talk with Luke since his dad's initial surgery. He was discouraged with how he had played and in actuality, felt he should not have played. I assured him that Dad would want him in and at the game. He would want Luke out there doing his part. The emotions were huge and Luke finally let himself fall into my arms and have a good cry. I realized at that moment how much all of this was on Luke. Because he was the only one at school that Friday, all of the questions from staff and students fell on him and he was pretty spent trying to be upbeat, but really not having any answers. And because I had been so busy at the hospital and with the girls, I had not spent any time with Luke one on one. It was a good moment of healing and really the only time I saw Luke be discouraged. For the most part he believed his dad would have a complete healing and be back on the court. I wasn't so convinced.

CHAPTER EIGHT

ON THE THIRD DAY

"The Lord has heard my supplication. The Lord receives my prayer." Psalm 6:9 NASB

January 13

On the first Sunday after the initial surgery, Greg was to go down to surgery for the first "wash-out" of his leg. Dr. Klaussen was on call that weekend and introduced himself to us. The girls and I, my sister Barb, our friends Pam and Kevin were there. It was strange because it was early morning, and we were the only ones in the waiting room. It was kind of a quiet, eerie feeling that morning reminding me of our first night there.

We had not taken time to eat breakfast, so Kevin took Amanda and went to get us all breakfast. The surgery went well. Dr. Klaussen said they would still need to watch the leg and see if circulation would be complete now that the muscles had space. I don't think I fully understood the real issues of the leg at that point. I was mostly concerned about all these open wounds vulnerable to infections. We desperately prayed there would be none.

That afternoon they were able to remove Greg's ventilator and he could speak in a whisper. It was the first time he could speak since Thursday night prior to the surgery. It was amazing how much he knew and remembered. We were able to answer questions and clarify things for Greg. He commented to us that he had probably given us a good scare. We said yes, he had!

His unit was a dark little cubby hole with no windows. On either side were people in pain and crisis and that was hard for him to listen to. Greg asked us about them, but of course we knew nothing of the other ICU roommates. It was just hard for him to listen to their pain. I knew that he would pray for them.

A steady stream of company showed up that day. I was rarely alone at the hospital, friends made sure I didn't sit by myself. Dave and Diane Parr were there early. They briefly greeted Greg, but mostly stayed by my side. I know they were always watching me, making sure I had what I needed, both physically and emotionally. They would assist me in greeting and visiting with others. What a help that was because I didn't have to tell everything to everybody. Having Barb there was great too. She took over some of the connections needing to be made.

It was interesting to see the mix of new friends and old friends, always intermingled with students. Past and present team members would stop by often and talk with me a little, wanting to know how Coach was that day. On that Sunday afternoon a group of four young men stopped by together. They, along with Luke, had been Greg's starting five when he coached them in their 7th and 8th grade season: Matt Whitaker, Aaron Sillanpa, John Parr, and Pete Newstrom. It was a pretty cool thing for them to do – to come together like that, showing solidly that they were pulling for Coach.

Sunday afternoon Pam took the girls and attended our 1:00 pm church service. I stayed at the hospital with friends and by Greg's side. When they came back, Pam asked if the kids and I wanted to come for supper. We decided that maybe we needed to get away and agreed to go. She was also having our friend Janet and her husband, Jonathan, for dinner. I had worked for Janet at our former church and had not seen her in nearly a year. Also there was Pam's precious Grandma Grace. She had all but adopted our family, so we had all come to call her Grandma. I remember I sat on the floor by her and she patted my head in comfort. She was just a special lady who I knew was praying for us and understood a lot of what I was going through.

We had dinner and I felt myself relax a little. It was good to catch up with Janet and Jonathan. They had been through some tough times, and I was glad to see how they were surviving. Janet and I understood each other well.

All of the sudden, after we'd finished eating, I had this urgent need to get back to the hospital. We always made sure the hospital knew how to reach us. They had our number, Pam's home and cell number and I always let them know where I would be. So even though there had not been any call, I just really needed to get back there. We bid our goodbyes and headed for the hospital.

When I arrived, there was no urgent need on Greg's part. He was stable and vitals were still good. But as I headed back for the waiting room, in walked my sister Gayle and brother-in-law Tim. They had just arrived in town coming from Iowa that day. I didn't know they were coming, but God alerted me to be there when they did. It was a great comfort to me to have them come. With them they brought a lot of well wishes from their church in Iowa with very kind notes from their parishioners, who were praying for us too.

I brought them into ICU to see Greg. He worked so hard to focus and know whom he was greeting. He thanked them for coming, calling them by name. I think Greg knew in that minute that the family really would take care of us. Tim spoke a prayer and we kissed Greg goodbye to head home. Everyone was always amazed how Greg knew who was there and how much, even while lying in that bed, he could give to them. It is just his nature to make people feel appreciated, and he was continuing to do that amidst his own frailty.

Heading home that night and having both my sisters with me was just great. It was very difficult for the kids and I to go home to that empty house with no Greg. I learned a lot during his hospital stay of what his presence brings to our home. It was empty without him.

The extra support of friends and family is so very helpful when you are in crisis. We apprised Gayle and Tim of Greg's current status and retold the story of the past four days. I knew Barb had been keeping in phone contact, but I also knew they wanted to check for themselves. Greg and I have spent a lot of time with their family in Iowa and know many of their friends. I knew that Tim and Gayle's church had encouraged them to come support us now.

CHAPTER NINE

A NEW WEEK

"Yet you do not know what your life will be like tomorrow..."
James 4:14 <small>NASB</small>

January 14

By now I had found the checkbook and Greg's wallet. I would teasingly thank him later that he had cash in his wallet for a change!

Greg always handled the finances and paying bills, but now I knew I needed to take a look at our current status. It was 5:00 am and I couldn't sleep. Not wanting to wake the others, I tiptoed around the house gathering what I would need to pay bills and sort mail. Back in my bedroom, I was again bewildered by the previous few days. It seemed like a bad dream, but each morning I awoke, it was our reality. Focusing on finances that morning gave me something to do, something else to think about while I waited for the family to awaken. I looked back at his payment dates and amounts and was able to sort it out and write a few bills.

I wrote out our regular payment to our dentist, who is also a very dear friend of ours, and planned to drop it off that morning. When we got to town, I did carry out my plan. After I parked the car, I ran into the dental office and said, "Here's my payment. Sorry I'm late!" I explained to them that Greg usually does bills and I was working on catching up with everything. Diane and Bev, the dental assistants, handed my envelope back to me. They told me I had no bill with them. I assured them, yes, I did and to please take the payment. They said they had hit the delete button on our bill. In their books, we were paid in full. I felt the tears coming and they told me not to cry, just to go take care of my husband. In the background Kim gave me half a smile and a nod. That was a $1200.00 bill, eliminated immediately. In tears I thanked them and headed across the street. I would thank Kim later when I saw him. From the start, he and his wife, LuAnn, would do anything to help us survive this crisis.

The day looked promising. Everything seemed to be progressing nicely. The doctors felt that after three more days in ICU Greg could go to his own room and in a week be home. So far, that was the most encouraging thing we had heard since the initial night of surgery that he had survived. Finally, something I could measure my life to. That Greg might be home in a week seemed and sounded wonderful. It felt so good to have the hope of something positive. We were all feeling much lighter.

I was always faced with the decision of who I should allow into ICU to see Greg. I didn't want to overburden him with company, yet I wanted him to know the kind of support that he and I had, and I felt he could really gain strength from men.

Mr. Terry Schoer, Greg's phy-ed buddy and office mate at the Marshall School, came that morning. I asked Terry if he wanted to see Greg. He said he did.

Not everyone is comfortable in a hospital and it can be difficult to see someone "down". So I always checked and asked, never assuming what anyone wanted or needed. It was good when they would be honest with me, either way.

I learned a lot about what men can bring and give to one another when a real need is felt. They can converse for days on end and never talk about anything really. But in a state of need, the words they bring and the thoughts they convey are marvelous. Mr. Schoer did that for Greg. For anyone who knew Greg, to see him on his back like that was overwhelming, but Terry really brought strength to Greg. His presence in the room confirmed in my heart, Terry was one person Greg needed to see.

Greg and Terry always refer to one another as Mr. Schoer and Mr. Mirau. It's just their way. It was special to hear Terry talk to Greg with the old familiar, yet comfortable title. He assured Greg he would be back, gave me a quick hug and headed back for school.

Coach Clark was another man who became an important visitor for Greg. The night before Greg became ill we had real concerns for Quincy, Coach Clark's son. Coach Clark had left practice early that Wednesday with our promise to pray for Quincy. I had gone to the boys' practice that evening because they were doing team photos. All the guys would be there and I wanted to take action shots of them for something I was making for the basketball banquet at the end of the year. As it worked out, Greg was able to be photographed with the team that night and assisted me in getting all the boys action photos taken. A day later and he would not have been there.

24 hours after our concern for Quincy, everyone focused on Greg. Coach Clark would come and grip Greg's hand, willing him to get well. He was amazed at Greg's focus on his son, Quincy, the dates, the games coming, etc. It became my pattern after watching these men in Greg's life to mostly bring men in to see Greg.

One day when Coach was at the hospital, he came and sat with me in the waiting room giving me a big hug, which wasn't like him. When I asked him teasingly why he was being so nice to me, he said, "I figure if Greg married you, there has to be something good there!" Coach Clark has become one of my favorite people through all of this, and he and Greg are very close friends.

I mentioned the Parr sons' visit on the first night we were at the hospital. The entire Parr family was really wonderful to us. We had developed a relationship through school and

Greg's role as Thomas and John's coach. It became the pattern of their dad, Dave, to spend most of everyday with me at the hospital. Between Dave, Pam, Teresa, Kim and LuAnn, and Kevin, I was rarely alone.

A few years earlier Dave had sat at a hospital waiting for his wife, Diane, to recover from brain surgery. Dave knew and understood a lot of what I was feeling. He also knew when to stay silent and when to have conversation. He became such a terrific listener and an interactive part of our whole journey. I am grateful to this man who sat with me day-by-day giving up so much of his own time to be there for us.

When Diane wasn't working she often came by, and she had a great way of analyzing the whole picture, asking good questions and giving me good counsel. I am glad to say they stayed with us the entire journey. Their counsel was invaluable.

That Monday morning, the doctors decided to get Greg out of bed for the first time. This became a much trickier proposition than normal because although they love to get heart patients up and going, Greg only had one leg to help them with, and the left leg had to stay elevated at all times. So they called in the "lift team". Before this, I never knew that the hospital had lift teams.

The lift team consisted of two big, strong, muscular guys who come and assist the nurses in the move. After a fair amount of effort, Greg was sitting up in a chair. The nurse came to get me after Greg was situated. I took Dave and Teresa in with me to see Greg. It was wonderful…but awful. Greg was exhausted from the effort, pale with the color draining from his face and barely had enough strength to hold his head up. Not the picture of health. He had been flat on his back for five days now and it is amazing how much strength you lose laying around. I was pulled between joy that he was sitting up and despair that he looked so very weak. We all encouraged and cheered him on, knowing that sitting in a chair was a victory in Greg's recovery journey.

Greg tired quickly. We visited a little bit, Greg always trying to piece together in his mind what had happened to his body. He was soon ready to go back to bed. To get him back in bed meant having to call the lift team back. Calling the lift team back meant waiting for them. They could be in any part of the hospital at any time. We learned to wait patiently for them.

CHAPTER TEN

LOSS

*"For He inflicts pain, and gives relief; He wounds,
and His hands also heal." Job 5:18 NASB*

January 15-16

It was Tuesday morning and this was our fifth day in the hospital. We knew that Greg had a scheduled "wash-out" of the leg that day. It was scheduled to happen fairly early in the morning so the girls and I were at the hospital ready and waiting. As much as possible, the girls were at the hospital during their dad's surgery times. Because of scheduling conflicts the surgery was delayed a couple of times. It was discouraging because we all wanted to be done with it. Greg's family had come down that day, knowing he was facing a surgery.

After the nurses learned that Greg was a coach, they would constantly put sports stations on TV, assuming that is what he would like. It was an okay effort, but Amanda went in that morning and turned on the Price Is Right, watching with her dad, trying to keep herself and her dad from worrying about the upcoming surgery.

Since surgery was delayed, Greg's family had a chance to visit with him before he was brought down to 4th floor. This was the first time they were able to speak with Greg and have Greg able to respond. Dr. Fetter came in while they were there and met them. He was explaining the initial surgery to Greg's family and why Greg would need to take coumadin from now on. Coumadin is a form of blood thinner which prevents blood from clotting on the new mechanical valve.

Greg would be on this, a multi-vitamin and a baby aspirin for the rest of his life.

A fair amount of people were in the waiting room of ICU bringing support and hope. We were seeing good, progressive signs. Greg's vitals were good, and he was hungry and beginning to eat solid food. We were all so encouraged and beginning to believe that we might survive this ordeal.

At about 11:30 am, Greg was wheeled down to surgery. As was our pattern we followed down to the 4th floor and the surgery waiting area. Greg's family, my sister Barb, who was still with us, my brother Gary, Pam and a few others waited while Amanda and I escorted Greg into the surgical pre-op room. This was the first time we had been in this pre-op space. It was so cold. When we asked about the coolness, they told us it was so the doctors would not sweat. The nurse brought Greg an extra blanket and then marked the leg that needed working on. In fact, she let Amanda mark it with a marker. It seemed so obvious to us what leg needed attention, but I guess it is a precautionary measure.

It was a strange experience to sit in that little holding space in pre-op listening to the conversations of other people waiting for surgery. The anesthesiologist came by and explained his role in the surgery, the medications being given, and so on. A nurse confirmed the surgery needed, and the leg it was to be done on. Amanda held up beautifully while sitting there. She talked with her dad, explaining to him what was coming and stroking his hand and face. It was amazing for me to watch her composure in there, chatting freely with her dad about school, friends, and what was happening in the upcoming surgery. We all looked around in disbelief at the space we were in and the fact that we had to be there. But taking it all in as a new experience helped fill some of the time.

72

When they were ready to take Greg into the surgery room, we kissed him goodbye, assuring him of our love and then exited to the waiting room and our waiting friends and family. It was there that Amanda just fell apart. I think it was Aunt Barb's arms that she fell into and just sobbed. All of the emotions that she controlled while she was with her dad came flooding out. I think it surprised her and I wondered if it had been too much for her to be in there. But I could not have deterred her. She had found a way to help and she was going to continue. So that strength she gave her dad was real and the breaking down afterwards was a pattern she repeated. She was an amazing 16 year old. I think the family just prepared themselves for her and always helped her bounce back up. I wonder what strength for the future she gained from that particular experience, actually from the whole experience. I'm sure as life goes on we will see it emerge again and again.

In the waiting room there was conversation flowing among family and friends, yet I sensed a real tension, too. I knew that I was exhausted so I let them carry on the conversations, half listening, half not. My heart and mind were with Greg and the surgeon. I knew they were watching carefully the muscles and tissues for infections and I continued to pray against any of those possibilities.

After an hour or so, Dr. Kaylor came to the waiting room to see us. He told us the surgery had gone well but that the muscle that lifts Greg's foot had died. In order to save the leg, it had to be removed. I remember the tears flowing at this news. Knowing Greg would be okay was wonderful, but there was a real grief knowing that the athlete in my husband had been forever changed. Joe, Greg's brother, said immediately, "Greg will handle it just fine. It will be okay." Dr. Kaylor explained briefly what this meant and that Greg would eventually be fitted with a brace. The leg would not be closed yet because they still had to watch it carefully for any more dead tissue. He told us that when it was closed, it would take a skin graft because the openings were so big. It would be able to be closed more quickly that way. At that point all I really heard was that we had several more surgeries ahead of us. It seems that some of the family asked Dr. Kaylor a few questions and he did some more explaining but I just remember the added weight I felt on my shoulders.

He left us and we all sighed, and then headed upstairs to ICU. I remember greeting a lot of people that day as they came and went. Pastor Ryan and Krista came. They assured me of their prayers and Krista said, "Greg will be healed and well in time for the revival." Pastor Ryan came into ICU with me and prayed for Greg, assuring him that his family was taken care of, that everyone was "loving on" them. Those words meant a lot to Greg and he squeezed Ryan's hand and nodded his thanks. It seemed like when Greg would begin to feel alert, another surgery would happen. Then he'd be exhausted from medications and the effort of his body trying to heal. Rest was what was needed.

But rest would not come easily that day. Because Greg was more alert now, they hooked him up to a button to give himself his own pain medication. The leg hurt terribly and he could not rest. Each time I would go in to see him, he would plead with me about the pain. I asked the nurses, but they just told me he could push the button when he needed pain relief. There seemed to be almost a "scolding" attitude among the nurses who seemed frustrated because we complained of the pain. It became a long agonizing day of watching him suffer, wincing with pain, and finding no solutions. And as long as he was hurting, he was not able to sleep.

Later in the day I spoke with Julie, who had been Greg's initial heart nurse. Julie was excellent in her approach and patient with my questions and my breakdowns. I felt that I could really trust her but right now, she wasn't Greg's nurse. Right now, the focus on Greg was concerning the leg. I remembered that a few days prior, Julie had spoken honestly with me telling me that Greg's condition was very serious, and there were beginning to be a lot of complications. But she reassured me saying she had seen people recover from worse, and that his healing was possible. Those were not easy words to hear, but I appreciated her being honest with me, not making any promises (which, of course, she couldn't), but also offering me reasons to hope.

Greg's nurse that day also tried to be helpful but for me really was not. It is a learning experience to be in a situation like this and observe how much personal opinion is offered. Her thoughts in trying to help me cope was to "prepare" me for what was coming. It was her opinion that because Greg had lost this muscle, our whole life would have to change. She told me that our family would have to redefine our roles. I could not expect my husband to be able to meet our needs and that I would need to be his caregiver. It was an awful moment for me. I wanted to deck her, but that wouldn't have done any good. She meant well, but that overload of data was not helpful and was not correct.

To be honest, Greg was in an ICU recovery room that was not really for leg issues. He was still there for his heart surgery recovery. In most cases a post-leg surgery patient would be placed on another floor. Because Greg had so many issues going on at once, he probably wasn't with people with the best information of post-leg care. It wasn't really anyone's fault, it was just the circumstances we found ourselves in. Greg's condition was multi-faceted, needing many areas of care.

I listened patiently to the nurse, but all I knew at that moment was that I felt a genuine grief for my husband. Greg was in horrible pain and I was tired. At about 6:00 pm, as became his habit, Scott Lucas, our dear friend (and clinical psychologist) came to the hospital to check on us. He worked at the adjoining clinic and would make daily treks after work to check on us. I was just coming out of ICU when he showed up. By now most of the friends had left and the evening group had not come by. I was alone and when he came I literally fell into his arms with tears. I could not take any more of Greg's suffering. Scott was wonderful that day. He went into Greg, spoke with him and then "used" his badge to get some action taken.

The first thing he assured me of was that pain was manageable and that Greg should not be hurting that much. Finally, someone who believed us. He spoke to the nurses explaining that Greg did not seem to be getting enough pain relief. He encouraged them to call the doctor and they were able to increase the pain medication. For the first time that day Greg felt relief from that horrible pain in his leg. Within a half hour Greg was finally able to sleep. I had become so drained trying to help Greg cope, I was barely able to think. It was an important moment and God's timing that brought Scott to my assistance right when I needed him.

Since Greg was now able to rest, I walked with Scott back to the clinic. These became daily walks for us as it gave me a chance to debrief my day. Free of charge! So much of the time spent in the hospital with friends and family is about helping them to understand, passing information, answering questions, and keeping others informed. I found that as wonderful as all of that was, those quiet walks with Scott allowed me to go deeper in my thought process. It was as if I could get outside of my circumstances and get a healthy look at what was happening. I still treasure those daily times and am so grateful for a friend who was also a listening ear at the end of a long day.

At this point people were already discussing how God was going to use this experience: what a testimony Greg would need to share, how we should think about using this in our lives, what it's purpose was. Scott gave me total freedom one night by saying that maybe this had no purpose at all. Maybe it just was what needed to happen. He encouraged me not to look ahead or to plan how it would be used, just to let it be. He helped keep me in the moment. I really didn't need to borrow tomorrow's worries. The day was filled with plenty of its own.

Luke had a basketball game that night that I planned on attending. I always made sure someone was at the hospital when I left. It was a tough decision for me each time, especially when the day had been difficult, which it was so many days. It was a difficult balance trying to maintain a normal schedule with Luke and the girls when nothing in our lives resembled normalcy. Luke was in his senior year; he, too, needed parental support. I did decide to attend all the in-town games knowing friends or family would stay near to Greg.

So this was the team's second game without their beloved coach. We had originally hoped to get the team, or part of them, in to see Greg within a week's time, but circumstances in Greg's healing prevented that possibility. Although I was exhausted from the very difficult day, I headed toward the school. I believed I could help keep the boys believing in themselves and ease their concerns about Greg if they saw me at the games. They played Central that night and lost by 10 points. They were trying, but it was hard. Pete N. told me that Coach Clark did a good job of helping them to spend time thinking about Coach Mirau and then helping to put it aside and play ball. After all, "That's what Coach Mirau would want you to do." His encouraging statements helped the guys some, but it was still hard not to think of Coach Mirau when he wasn't there where he belonged. Coach Clark told me that as often as possible, they left Greg's chair on the bench "open," none of them ever totally letting go of their thoughts of Greg.

As was the case on many evenings, when we arrived home there was a barrage of messages on the answering machine but we were too tired to return them. So we would make a list of the names and numbers and Pam, who became my personal secretary, began the task of returning calls. She was fantastic, introducing herself by phone to people she didn't know, explaining her role as my friend, and giving people the updates. I know she even gave out her number so people could call her instead of us. What a great ministry that was to the kids and I. It was another way to relieve the stress and pressure on our family.

One of the ladies she called was from the Mahtowa Covenant Church where Greg does lay preaching. She and Hulda became friends by phone, and I still don't think they have ever met. I know that the whole body of Mahtowa Church was praying to God and those updates from Pam kept them well informed. In the first few days of our hospital stay, the church in Mahtowa delivered a gift certificate to the hospital restaurant to assist us with meals. It was a very thoughtful gesture.

Wednesday morning Greg seemed more rested than he had for a long time. With the extra pain relief he was able to sleep as well as anyone can in ICU. If you're not familiar with ICU, they check on you constantly so there is a lot of interruptions. At about 9:30 I was sitting with Greg, catching up on Luke's game, etc. when Dr. Kaylor came in. He said hi to us both and then he looked at me and asked me if I had told Greg what had taken place in surgery yesterday. I shook my head a little and said no. He said, "That's fine, I'll tell him." He proceeded to explain to Greg how the muscle that lifts the foot had died, and that they had removed it. He told Greg that he would be fitted with a brace eventually to help with the lift and assured him that it would not affect the strength of the leg. The tears just flowed from me, but Greg squeezed my hand and said it would be okay. We'll handle it. I will say this, Greg was very positive through this whole journey.

Throughout our journey, so many wonderful people came to the hospital to check on Greg and our family. People I didn't expect, or that I didn't know even knew what was going on. Each day I would be amazed by who would come around that corner. Like I said, our support system was incredible.

When Coach Clark came that evening I told him what had happened with Greg's leg and what it would mean. He said to me, "That won't bother Greg, he'll just slap on the brace and say 'let's go.' " I appreciated Coach at that moment because his comment helped me step back and see the whole picture and also helped me remember who Greg was, the kind of man he was. Sometimes I became so afraid in the moment that I could not see past it. Those kinds of comments usually helped me to refocus. It was a good thing that Coach had come by.

Another family was also in our waiting room on the 7th floor on a regular basis. Elsie became a good friend, as well as her daughter and sons. Her husband was in ICU because of a surgery gone badly, and his system was getting poisoned. I felt great empathy for her and the difficult news they had to bear on and off; she felt it for me because Greg was young and we had three kids bearing this load who were still in high school. We formed a strong bond and friendship. It was neat because she met many of our friends, and they too reached out to Elsie and her family.

One day in particular stands out. Greg was stable that day, but her husband John was not. I went over to her as she was crying and asked if I could pray for her. She said yes and the friends who were with me rallied around Elsie as we lifted up John to the Lord. John had entered the hospital the same day as Greg, and on many levels would follow our course through the hospital, although his hospital stay would be even longer than Greg's.

In the meantime, Dr. Fetter was lobbying for us to move Greg to a different unit. The room we were in had no windows and was very close to the noisy nurses' desk. A unit became available, so while he was sitting up that day they prepared the room for him. This forced him to stay upright a little longer than usual, but the room with a view was a nice change. He was so tired; he could hardly keep his head up waiting for the change. The room was a little farther away from the nurses' station and the busyness of the unit. There was a glass door that could be closed and his room could be kept quieter. I was grateful for the move, because even though we did not know it at the time, he was to be in that room for a long time.

CHAPTER ELEVEN

BLACK THURSDAY

"Your words have helped the tottering to stand, and you have strengthened feeble knees. But now it has come to you, and you are impatient; it touches you, and you are dismayed."
Job 4:4-5 NASB

January 17

Thursday, January 17th came with the knowledge that there was yet another "wash-out" of the leg. It was scheduled for around 11:00 am. When I arrived at the hospital that morning I was told immediately that the night had not gone well. Greg's hemoglobin had dropped and he was receiving two units of blood. They were hopeful to be able to close the outside of the leg, but would not know until they looked at it. Since the last "wash-out" had resulted in a leg muscle being removed, we were a little anxious about this one. Our hope was that this surgery would be routine. The blood loss could easily have been related to the open wounds of the leg. We were pretty confident that it was not related to the initial heart surgery. Since Greg's second surgery to stop the bleeder, that had not been a real concern for us.

This was Greg's sixth surgery. We had been in the hospital for one week. Our spirits began to sag a bit, but if the leg could be closed that would be a huge victory. I still was not able to comprehend all that was happening to Greg and our family. I never had any time to digest it. Many others shared the same disbelief. It was as if it were a bad dream, and I just could not wake up. I really wanted to wake up! But reality has a way of just hitting you in the face and making you face the moment. This was not a dream, it was our lives.

The surgery seemed to go fine with no major complications. Dr. Kaylor had found no dying muscles, and any dead tissue debris had been "washed out". After Dr. Kaylor left us, we went back upstairs to our "corner" of the hospital. A lot of people were there that day and we were busy updating everyone on the current status, explaining that although the wash out had gone well, they still had not been able to close the wounds. Until they were closed, we knew there would be more surgeries. Dr. Fetter came by to see us, having checked on Greg himself, knowing the leg surgery was completed. He, too, assured us everything looked good and went well. Even though these leg surgeries were not Dr. Fetter's area, he was always close by and kept up-to-date on Greg's status. He was encouraged and talked with me about moving Greg out of ICU, perhaps as soon as the next day.

There had been considerable discussion among the doctors as to where Greg should go for continued care: the heart unit or the orthopedic unit. Both areas of Greg's body needed continual care. It was decided that the 6th floor, the heart unit, would be best. Dr. Fetter was working on securing a private room on the 6th floor for Greg. Greg could get continued heart care with nurses who understood the heart surgery recovery area and what was needed. The orthopedic people and rehab people could come to Greg there and do their things, hopefully beginning some leg rehabilitation.

The waiting room, as usual, was full of friends and family and we were all happily and hopefully listening to Dr. Fetter's plans for Greg's move. While Dr. Fetter was speaking to me about all this, he was paged. He excused himself and left. I knew what a busy doctor he was, and always appreciated the extra time he gave us while respecting his need to attend to many other patients. Moments later the nurse from ICU came out to speak to me. She pulled me aside in a quiet space in the hospital hallway. She said I needed to go to the 4th floor

82

surgery waiting room, offering no details on why I was needed there, only that there was a complication. I felt tears threatening to push up inside of me, but I pulled myself together and went back to face my support group. I told them that although I had no information, I needed to go to the 4th floor waiting room. I selected three people to go down with me. My brother Gary, my future brother-in-law Rod, and Pam. We headed down with no idea why we were being asked to go there, but a fear was welling up inside of me.

As soon as I gave my name to the volunteers of the waiting room, I could tell they were expecting me. They directed us to a private waiting room and asked us to wait there for the doctor. In a few minutes Dr. Fetter arrived. His pager had gone off because of Greg.

Shortly after the surgery, which had gone very well, Greg was brought to post-operative recovery room. A routine procedure. It was while he was in OR recovery that Greg's body went into crisis. The sack around Greg's heart began to fill with fluid or blood. The compression caused by the fluid would not allow the heart to pump with full force. Dr. Fetter needed me to sign more release papers for him to go in and surgically relieve that pressure and insert drainage tubes. They had to give Greg's heart immediate release from the fluid that was threatening his recovery. Through tears I signed the papers. Dr. Fetter told me Greg's situation was like a commercial he had seen for a movie where a person was going down a slide and it never ended, it just kept going and going. I remember my heart pounding loudly and my spirit crying for release. I was so weary of things going wrong. We did not need any more bad news.

He left us to do the needed surgery and I remember weeping and asking, "Why is this happening to Greg?" I felt beside myself with fear and grief. Pam led us in prayer. At that moment, it felt like this journey would never end. Why did complications keep happening?

We sat in that little room a few minutes while I tried to gain my composure. I could see on the face of my brother Gary, Rod, and Pam a real sharing of the concern and heartache. I knew what and whom I had to face upstairs: the girls and friends were up there waiting for us. I gave a brief update to our little support group, my daughters and friends, sharing the latest update. I dreaded having to give the girls the news. They were as tired as I of the whole ordeal.

Amanda and Abbey both began to cry. Abbey left the room; she had found a special place to go, sit, and be alone up on the 10th floor. I let her go, knowing she had to face her own grief and fears. Someone placed their arms around Amanda and me, and we wept quietly.

I remember Meg Lucas had come that day, and I had no energy to visit with her. I know she didn't mind. There were probably others that day that I gave nothing to, but I also knew they were there to help me, not me them.

Dr. Fetter said he would find us in the ICU waiting room after he was done in surgery. It was awhile before he came and explained the surgical procedure that had been completed.

The operative report I later received stated: "We cut the old sutures from the lower part of the sternal wound. Once we cut through the linea alba layer, there was evidence of a fair amount of fluid under pressure and this was drained. Once we cut through the linea alba interrupted Vicryl stitches, we drained approximately 800cc of fluid. The patient did have some slight improvement in his blood pressure and his heart rate did slow down from about 110 to 106, but there was no real dramatic improvement. We then placed two drainage tubes, one next to the diaphragm and one in front of the heart. We then […] closed the rest of the incision […] a sterile dressing was applied and the patient was transferred to the Intensive Care Unit...."

They had placed drainage tubes in Greg and had drained a quart of fluid from Greg's chest. That was a lot of fluid to gather around the heart. Dr. Fetter wasn't sure what had happened to cause that much fluid to gather around the heart so quickly. Greg was placed back on a ventilator to assist with his breathing and he was heavily sedated. They brought him back up to his unit in ICU.

After he was done speaking to me, Dr. Fetter faced the girls and spoke with them. I'll never forget his crouching down in front of Abbey and really giving her time and attention, offering to re-explain what was happening, and answering any questions. I know she asked a couple of questions and I think at that moment she became his fan. This very busy surgeon was also a dad and understood well the pain in this daughter. It was a wonderful thing he did at that moment, taking time and placing value on the little things.

How it felt to go in and see Greg that night will probably never be erased from my mind. Matt, my nephew, went in with me. There was no need for a parade of people, Greg was heavily sedated and would not know we were there.

As I stood with tears and fear, Matt holding on to me, Dr. Fetter came and spoke to us. He asked me whose Bible was lying there by Greg's bed and I told him Amanda had brought her Bible for her dad. He opened it and read scripture to us, helping us to hold on to the promises of God. And then he said, "Robynne, we are a long ways away from hopeless. Greg is critically, critically, critically ill. But we are a long ways away from hopeless. If we get close to hopeless, I'll let you know." These were powerful, personal words from a physician who became our number one supporter. I stood at the end of Greg's bed watching over his struggling body feeling like my world was falling apart. We were back to square one, unable to speak with Greg, and having so many monitors around him. All of the progress I felt we were making seemed to diminish.

I could barely stand to look at my husband at this point. I felt so wounded inside. I know I leaned a lot on Matt. We turned to leave Greg's unit, and I know as we walked out of there, Matt was amazed by our surgeon who had spoken those words. This doctor who had taken the Word of God and read to us, who in the midst of a horrible crisis, still gave us something to hold on to, a reason to hope. I was trying to hold on to those words.

I wondered if this would be the way God would take Greg's life. Had the physical battles become too complicated and too grave to recover from? A nurse was placed in his room to monitor him non-stop. The night had suddenly become very, very dark.

When Kevin and Scott L. came by that night we shared the disastrous updates of the day. Their hearts, too, were burdened with the difficulties of the day. Before we left that evening Kevin stood with me by Greg's side, silently watching the ventilator helping Greg to breathe. With an arm on my shoulder and his other hand in Greg's, Kevin led in prayer, willing for Greg's life and the children and me. I know at that moment his heart was as heavy as mine.

We headed home late that night, extremely exhausted and wishing we could put an end to the nightmare we were living. It had been such a hard day. Pam would later call it "Black Thursday". I was so overwhelmed by the weight of the burden of that day. I told Teresa it would be easier to let God take Greg, rather than to continue to watch him suffer. It hurt so much to see the suffering Greg was forced to endure. It broke my heart to realize how many backward steps we had taken that day.

CHAPTER TWELVE

FRIENDS, IN THE TIME OF NEED

"Rejoice with those who rejoice, and weep with those who weep."
Romans 12:15 *NASB*

January 18-19

On Friday morning we were somewhat encouraged. The nurses said Greg had rested well through the night, and that his vitals had remained stable. The doctors told me they felt he had turned a corner. I think what the doctors were pleased about was the stability of Greg's vitals through the night, and that they had immediately been able to respond to the crisis before it was too late. I held a small hope that the real healing would begin now, and that the hits of bad news were over.

The inquiries about Greg continued with more and more first time visitors. Dr. Fetter said each morning as he parked his car at work and walked into the hospital he was barraged with many questions from other doctors who knew Greg and who were looking for answers. Of course he was not at liberty to speak about his patient, only to say Greg was stable. He told me that morning, "Greg is more popular than the mayor; I'm a fan of his too."

In the meantime, God had spoken to Pam and told her she needed to fight with prayer what was happening in Greg's life. She always looks back on that Thursday as the hardest day in our journey. But God used the fear and seriousness of Greg's situation to speak to Pam, and she got on the phone and rallied friends to come and pray.

Greg's morning nurse, Arlee, came out to see me. She told me that she felt Greg was discouraged and down and that he needed to talk with me. She also felt that he wanted to protect me and be strong. She assured him I was strong enough and to trust me to help him. She was, in retrospect, one of Greg's favorite nurses.

I went in to Greg and tried to communicate with him. The communication was very difficult. Greg could not talk because of the ventilator. He was pointing with his hands outside the window, downward. To be honest, I was absolutely horrible in trying to understand him. At one point I thought he was telling me he had a dream. I asked him if he saw heaven; he shook his head no. Then I asked him if he saw hell (he was pointing downwards after all). He looked at me with startle in his eyes, and then I quickly realized he would not see hell; Jesus lived in his heart. After much struggle, I got the message from him that he would like to see his friend Kim. Kim is our dentist, right across the street from the hospital. I said I would go and ask him to come.

As I entered the office, Kim's assistants were great. I told them that Greg was asking for Kim. Kim stepped out of a dental room and I told him what I needed. He asked if he could finish the root canal he was working on, then he would be right over. I teased him that I thought he had a priority problem, finishing his work before he saw Greg. I went back and let Greg know Kim would come as soon as he could.

In the meantime, my brother Clyde and his wife Roxy came. Clyde and Greg have a special bond; they just connect. I shared with them the difficult day before and the complications that were upon us. Clyde is a lumberjack; he spends a lot of time in the woods working alone. But as he went in to see Greg with me it was amazing. He took Greg's hand in his own and told him he knew he had had a difficult time in the past 24 hours. Greg would communicate with hand gestures and Clyde understood. What I could not do well with my husband, Clyde was able to do. Some things were not easy to understand and we finally got a pen and notepad.

With difficulty, laying on his back, Greg was able to write small notes to aid him in saying what he wanted. It was a blessing to see how much Clyde understood Greg and what comfort it brought to Greg. Greg could just write a word, and that would be enough for Clyde to converse with him. As I stood and watched them communicate, Clyde told Greg, "You're on a journey and this is a big bend in the road, but we're coming around that bend. You are going to make it, and then the road will straighten out. You hang in there. Just a little longer." Tears flowed from my eyes to hear my brother speak to my husband that way.

I lifted my head and outside of Greg's unit was his friend Mike and wife Julie. I went to Mike who was sobbing. They had heard that Greg was dying and his heart was torn in two. I told him that Greg had stabilized through the night and though he was back on the ventilator, he was doing okay.

I led Mike out of the ICU unit, leaving Greg in the capable hands of my brother. I was stunned to see the hallway lined with people, so many people who came to pray – UMD students, (Pastor Ryan told me he could have brought many more), family, friends, neighbors. They had gathered there to pray for Greg. It was a powerful and awesome moment for me to see my family gathered with friends, gathered with college students. I greeted each with a hug and took Mike to a quiet corner. As they prayed I tried to comfort and console Mike. I think there was just so much Mike wanted to have a chance to say to Greg, and he was afraid he would not get a chance. Because Greg was so ill, I suggested that Mike write Greg a note and assured him I would give it to Greg. Mike did write a wonderful note, expressing much of what he needed to say to Greg. That note is still in my hospital journal, a treasure for Greg to have always.

Meanwhile, Kim had come over from his office and was part of the prayer team. He then went in to see Greg. He too had an uncanny ability to understand Greg. Greg scribbled on a note to Kim that he loved him and called him his friend. Kim returned that support and brought strength to Greg. It was a very good thing and what Greg needed that day.

What my brother and Kim brought to Greg that day confirmed in my heart that men could really minister to Greg. That somehow, unexplainable on some levels, Greg could draw inner strength from the men in his life he is close to. I know Greg was comfortable with them and really let them help him.

Dr. Mark Eckman, an infectious disease specialist, and also a Marshall School parent, was brought in as a consultant on Greg's case because of a spiking fever and possible infections. His consult report dated January 17, 2002 refers to Greg's case as follows "...I have known (him) for several years since my son played basketball under his tutelage. I am seeing him today as a consequence of fever and after a rather disastrous week which will be summarized with problems below." It had been a disastrous week.

There is quite a summary in that report with more medical terminology than I would ever care to know. Dr. Eckman goes on to state, "Greg has been an exemplary human being with a strong Christian faith, and has an extremely caring attitude as a coach. Because of the number of people he has touched, visitors have had to be restricted."

Later that day they diagnosed Greg with having ARDS, Adult Respiratory Distress Syndrome. There was a fever again and with the ARDS they felt they needed to keep him on the respirator. Greg was very uncomfortable with it and wanted to take it out. He would occasionally pull at it and so they were forced to tie his hands down. I cannot tell you how difficult that was to see and deal with. Since he was on the ventilator and could not talk, he did not want to lose the use of his hands. I think he was angry inside and he became more restless. We all tried to verbally reassure him and help him to be patient. To tell him to be patient was easy for us to say as we all had our freedom. It was much more difficult for Greg to bear.

On Saturday, the fever was continuing. Greg's vitals were good, everything from his initial surgery seemed right on track with healing, but the nagging fever would not end. Surgery number eight was scheduled for that morning – another "wash out" of the leg. I was hoping and praying that Greg would be able to get off the ventilator that day; it was so uncomfortable for him.

The days really started to drag, they were long and hard with very little good news. There wasn't a bunch of bad news, just not much progress. Each day we would help Greg get oriented by telling him the day, the date, the time and what was going to happen that day.

Despite the fever, they did the scheduled surgery and it went well. The 2nd muscle they were concerned about looked good. It appeared to have survived the compartment syndrome pressure. They were hopeful to be able to close the leg in a day or two. That night, prayer support came and stood outside Greg's room in the form of Kim and LuAnn and Kevin. I was to learn later that Cindy S. from the Marshall School would also come and stand outside of ICU and pray. Only the Lord knows how many others rallied with us in prayer. We were grateful for each one.

Kim Chart had come that morning and taken my van keys. I had joked with him about washing it sometime for me. Well, he did that day: washed, vacuumed, oil change, and a new battery for the remote. When he came back that evening I could see the weight on his shoulders. He had been in to see Greg and the strain was so great. He tearily handed me my keys and an envelope of cash stating he had "robbed the bank." I hugged him and thanked him. I reminded him how much Greg loved him and tried to encourage him to believe that Greg would recover. We walked arm in arm to the entrance of the hospital sharing a heavy load in our hearts. LuAnn told me later that Kim wanted to do so much for Greg, even thinking he should take him to the Mayo Clinic in Rochester, MN. I have a deep appreciation for Kim and Lu and the huge amount of burden they carried for our family. It spoke of a great love.

LuAnn came one day and said after visiting with Greg she just wanted to hug him, but there was no way with all the wires, the ventilator and the tubes, so she had given him a kiss on the forehead. She wanted to be sure that was okay. I assured her to kiss him all she wanted. I believed Greg needed all the touching and affirming we all could give.

CHAPTER THIRTEEN

MARSHALL MEDICAL MEN

*"It is not those who are healthy who need a physician,
but those who are ill." Matthew 9:12* NASB

January 20-21

On Sunday, January 20th, we marked Greg's 10th day in
ICU. It had been a very long stretch. There was no surgery
scheduled for that day, but we did learn that the ventilator
would have to stay in at least another 24 hours. The lungs
were still cloudy from the ARDS. The doctor took me over and
showed me the x-rays and pointed to what their concerns
were. Even I could see the cloudiness in the lungs.

As stated earlier, Dr. Eckman became Greg's infectious
disease specialist to assist with the infection. His son, James,
had been at Marshall and under Greg's coaching so Dr.
Eckman was eager to help. Dr. Eckman had stopped by to
see me one day because his wife had told him, "You find Mrs.
Mirau and find out what's happening." The next day he was
"on the case". I am very grateful for all Dr. Eckman did for
Greg; he had to do an amazing amount of work and prescribe
incredibly strong antibiotics to try and assist with Greg's
healing.

Dr. Mike Maddy, also a Marshall parent, came on as the
kidney specialist. They reduced Greg's fluid intake to help the
lungs improve. The excess fluid Greg had was putting a strain
on the kidneys. It became a difficult balance for the doctors.
At one point Greg was near renal failure, something I didn't
know until much later.

When Greg was alert he would pull on the ventilator. To
have it put back in was very difficult and uncomfortable for

him. Amanda would tell her dad not to touch it and he would look at her with scolding eyes. It was a comical moment, but also trying. But in those moments and in trying to assist her dad with recovery, Amanda would be the parent, telling her dad what to or not to do. Because Greg was so uncomfortable and restless and pulling on the respirator, they decided to put him in a drug-induced coma.

Now that Greg was sleeping most of the time, our communication with him really dwindled. We missed him reaching his hand towards us and telling him stories of our day. It was really hard to have him sleeping most of the time. Although it was necessary, it felt like he was so much farther away because of it. We could only call his name and have him lift his sleepy eyes toward us. The girls commented on how far away he looked, even when he opened his eyes. Nevertheless, we let him know we were there, stroking his forehead and arms. In our hearts we felt the deeper separation. We did not have Greg's presence at home and now we had lessened our connection with him at the hospital. The progress was slow, but the medical staff assured me he was improving, albeit at the pace of a turtle.

Our stay in the ICU was once again prolonged. I remember asking a girlfriend of mine who is a nurse, how do people do after so many days in ICU? She wasn't sure; she stated most people don't stay there this long. I knew with the constant lights, interruptions, noise, that days and nights were very confusing to Greg. Maybe now that he was only resting, the confusion wouldn't be so bad when he was awakened.

Each day was long and the week that Greg was in the induced coma made me feel somewhat useless. It was great that he was resting. I would go in and wake him a little to let him know I was there and that I loved him. The nurses would give me an update of the night and we all would pray. Each morning I would check all the monitors, seeing the numbers, reading the charts.I was always glad that the heart remained steady, no glitches there. It was one thing to really hold on to.

Some mornings I would have quiet time before other visitors came and it was a good moment to pray and reflect. I had begun a journal on Greg's 3rd day in the hospital, listing visitors, phone calls and a brief medical update for the day. I am glad now that I did that; I never could have kept track of all the events otherwise. Journaling allowed me to pen down on paper each day's events, and also freed my mind from having to keep all the details straight. People asked a lot if they could look at it; it helped many sort out the days and events.

Because Greg needed rest, I would not stay in his unit very long. If I were there he would work too hard to be awake and then be aware of the ventilator and struggle more with being uncomfortable. So I spent a lot of my time in the ICU waiting room, visiting with the company that always came. I would enter the ICU unit fairly often to check on Greg and to be with him, then quietly slip away so he could rest. Almost always when I went back out to the waiting area, there was someone new to talk with. We had both light moments and very heavy moments in that room where we spent so many hours.

I would sit back and marvel at how people introduced themselves to each other and made connections and friendships with people they hadn't met before. My family became acquainted with just about everyone Greg and I knew. I began to get this really uneasy feeling in my spirit. Something was very strange. I talked with Scott Lucas about it that night in our walk time and he wasn't sure what I was feeling and I really wasn't able to describe it to him.

There had been a lot of discussion of how this event would be used in our lives or in others and Scott thought maybe I was taking on the weight of planning tomorrow's events. I listened, but wasn't convinced that this what was causing the restlessness inside me. I needed to think about it some more.

A day later I was able to identify it. In our "normal lives" our whole world comes together for our wedding and our funeral. When you get married you invite everyone you know. They all gather for the ceremony and celebration. They may meet a few new people, spend a couple of hours together, then they go their own way. For the most part the only one who knows everyone are the bride and groom. At funerals, the setting is the same, the gathering of the people who know you.

But here we were, mid-stream of life, and all of a sudden everyone we knew was showing up for a gathering. And it wasn't just for a few hours or days. It became many days. I realized the uneasiness I was feeling was because all of my boundaries of relationships were being broken down. Everyone was meeting everyone and building new relationships. I began to feel like I was losing safe zones. For most of us this type of moment never happens. It isn't really a good or bad thing, just very unusual. I found I didn't need to introduce people or anything. They had already met and would be catching up on a previous conversation. It was absolutely incredible to watch. These are people who are supposed to be strangers to each other, with no reason in the world to meet. They were brought together, not just for a moment, but also for a journey as we anticipated Greg's healing.

Greg had been in ICU now for a long time. We had watched other patients come and go, but still John (Elsie's husband) and my Greg remained there. Originally we had hoped that the basketball team could come by and see Greg in four to five days. As things kept going wrong, we kept having to tell them they just could not come. Coach Clark came by regularly and would receive the update to report to the team. I always let him see Greg for a moment and bring encouragement. He would stand by Greg's side carrying on one-sided conversations, updating Greg on Quincy and the team's progress, or lack thereof.

CHAPTER FOURTEEN

THE LAST SURGERY

"Whoever is wise, let him understand these things. Whoever is discerning, let him know them. For the ways of the Lord are right, and the righteous will walk in them." Hosea 14:9a NASB

January 22-23

During Greg's illness the basketball team really struggled. How could they not? How were they supposed to concentrate on basketball when in the back of their minds was the concern that their coach could die? I believed that if they could only see him, it would help so much, but it just wasn't feasible yet. I knew at practices Luke would try to keep it positive, focusing on what was going right for his dad. But it was hard to keep on hoping when so many days brought difficult, negative turns.

On Tuesday, January 22nd, Greg was scheduled for another surgery. He was still running a fever, which concerned the doctors, but the other vitals were good. How many times did I stand in his room and watch all the monitors, his pulse, heart rate, blood pressure – the buzzing and the beeping of an ICU unit? Nothing ever really alarmed anyone, just that constant nagging fever. Greg was placed on some strong antibiotics to fight any potential infection.

We were now facing Greg's ninth surgery when we still had not fully processed in our hearts his first surgery. My brother, Clyde, and his wife, Roxy, had come that day. My friend Jan and her husband, Jerry, had come by with cookies. We were visiting in the ICU waiting room when the nurse summoned me that we were headed downstairs for surgery. I bid Jan and Jerry a quick good-bye and with my entourage of support headed for surgery waiting, a now way too familiar place. Laurie West and Pam were there along with my brothers Clyde, Dave, and Gary. I remember saying that I could hardly believe we were heading for a ninth surgery. Roxy looked at me and said with confidence, "This will be his last." I wasn't so sure. But I saw a knowing in her that day; she really believed what she had said. Somehow, she knew.

As we sat there waiting for Dr. Kaylor to come, LuAnn Chart came, having picked up Abbey from school for me. We updated her and Abbey on what we knew and they joined us in the wait. Abbey was sitting on the floor doing homework when Dr. Kaylor came out and told us the leg looked good and that surgery had gone well. He told us they had been able to do the skin grafts and close the open wounds on Greg's leg. He explained to us that you can tell within a few minutes if a graft would "take" or not and that Greg's looked good. Greg's legs were grafted closed! This for us was a huge victory because we were all so concerned about infections getting into those open wounds. He answered questions that people had and then went to leave, stepping over Abbey's legs. Then he paused and bent down to talk with her a moment, checking on what she was studying. It meant so much to me when the doctors saw people, saw our lives and took those moments, especially for my kids. I am sure those direct moments between the doctors and my kids, even though brief, were vital for my kids surviving the crisis of their dad's.

Because of the longevity of Greg's care, the medical staff put him on a special bed. It was air inflated and could be set to rotate up and down. They felt this would help with breathing and the healing of his lungs. It also helps with circulation and in the reduction of bedsores. Greg was constantly on his back, unable to move with the leg in such a crisis.

Luke and Amanda were headed with the basketball team that afternoon to Mesabi East, Greg's old alma mater. I wanted the kids to know that their dad had come through his final surgery and that the graft had been completed. Pam called Greg's mom so she could get a message to them since she would be at the game that night. We also called the school, and Pam asked if there was any way to let Luke and Amanda know. The school called the bus company, who called the bus driver, who handed the phone to Coach Clark, who relayed the message to the kids on the way to the game. It was a good moment for Luke and Amanda and for the team. A surge of victory! Coach Mirau had survived the final surgery. Now maybe everything could begin to go right and be a little easier.

It did not help the team as much as I would have hoped. They lost that night. I think their hearts were still too heavy. But they played hard and were still working on being a winning team. Coach Radzak told me later that he had scouted the Mesabi East team and knew Marshall had a very good chance of winning. But Coach Clark said that even though they should have won, the boys just played terribly. He felt because it was Greg's alma mater and they all knew it, it probably put the presence of Greg's battle right on top of the team's heart, and they just could not focus. Dan B. told me he always wondered why they could not focus. He knew they had the talent, they had confidence, where was the focus? He later concluded it was because a "piece of the puzzle was missing" – Coach Mirau.

A lot was happening with the team during this time. Coach Clark and the team all said that their perspective on winning or losing had changed. It wasn't that they didn't want to win, but now losing had a totally different feel to it. It just was not as important. Coach Clark told me he use to get down after a loss, but now the basketball battle seemed minor compared to the battle for Greg's life. His focus and that of the whole team took on a different perspective.

On Wednesday morning Greg's condition was stable, but he was still fighting a fever. The doctors were still unsure of the reason. The leg looked good and the vitals were steady, yet still the fever continued. Our hopes of removing the ventilator were not to be realized yet. Until they could remove the ventilator, they were not going to wake him up.

The nurses showed us the graft sites on Greg's left leg. To the girls and I they looked horrible, blood oozing on his thigh from the donor site and tubes draining from the graft area. They placed a "tent" over Greg's legs because they could not allow any material to touch the new surgery sites. I think this time was as hard as the ARDS evening when the chest had filled with fluid.

I stood by Greg's side, looking at all the scars, trying to comprehend how much had happened to Greg's body in eleven days. It was so overwhelming! His chest had a long incision and there were drainage tube sites below that. They had surgically implanted an intravenous site on the upper left side of the chest. The groin would bear a new scar, plus the two leg incisions and now the graft site on his thigh. It looked as if he had been in a horrible accident when in fact, each incision was an attempt to save his life. It was so overwhelming to my heart. There were no choices, only necessary surgeries. My heart went from heavy grief of all the scars to a guarded relief that maybe we were done with surgery. I just knew that I felt very, very heavy inside.

I realized in this time how much I took for granted from my husband. I just always got strength from him, and he from me. It was a part of our marriage. But now, as he lay there, strength had to come from God and from within. Having children depend on you alone sure matures a person. I have a real respect for single parents; it is a tough job.

A friend from a church where Greg had served as a youth pastor came by and saw me that day. She had a cash gift for the kids and I. She wanted me to know she was praying and they would do anything they could to help us. It was very kind; I had not seen her in many, many years. These random visits from people in our past really impacted me and Greg later when he heard about them. It is a real act of compassion to make that extra effort to see someone you have not seen in a while.

It was amazing how people from our past appeared at the hospital. I came out of ICU one evening and a man was sitting there visiting with my sister and her husband. She asked if I knew who he was. I didn't recognize him, but he introduced himself. He and Greg had been in a band together some 25 years ago. He said he didn't want to see Greg, just wanted to be near.

The finance person from Marshall also came to speak with me. She gave me the update on our financial status with the school. Fortunately, Greg was never sick and had accumulated a lot of sick days. We needed them. She wanted me to know they were beginning the paperwork for disability pay for Greg. I told her I didn't believe he would need that, but she felt they should begin the process. She would send me the paperwork in the mail. I thanked her but in my heart I hated that conversation. To make preparations that maybe Greg wouldn't be back at Marshall for me was unthinkable. I just could not go there.

CHAPTER FIFTEEN

THE POWER OF THE PRAYING PASTOR

"...and the prayer offered in faith will restore the one who is sick, and the Lord will raise him up..." James 5:15a NASB

January 23-24

That evening, Pastor Ryan came and we updated him on the victory in surgery that day. He was pleased to learn that Greg had finished his last surgery. I took him in to see Greg. He assured Greg in his sleepy state that he was praying for him, everyone was watching over Greg's family, and encouraged Greg to just rest and get better. Then he told Greg he would pray for him. He began to pray holding Greg's hand in his own and placed his other hand on me. While he prayed Greg's bed began to move (remember he was on that special air mattress). Well, I had failed to mention the new bed to Ryan. So while he was praying Ryan felt Greg pulling up to him. He had to open his eyes, because for a moment, he thought maybe Greg really was rising out of bed! It was a comical moment. Ryan continued to pray and talked openly and honestly with God about Greg's condition. A powerful prayer.

The ICU was still staffing Greg's room continually because of the critical nature of his battles. The nurse, of course, heard Pastor's prayer. After Pastor Ryan had left she pulled me aside and asked me if I didn't think that kind of praying would just upset the patient. I looked at her and said, "Not this man, he thrives on that. That kind of praying is a blessing to my husband's heart." It amazed me to know that that kind of praying had impacted her.

Thursday morning brought more tough news. It appeared that Greg had developed a touch of pneumonia. They assured me the internal medicine doctors were on it, placing Greg on antibiotics to fight against the pneumonia. They were also beginning a process of weaning Greg from the ventilator. They would turn the ventilator off for short periods of time, forcing Greg to breathe on his own. He seemed to tolerate more and more of the breathing on his own. It was a good sign.

By Friday, the antibiotics were doing their job; the fever was reduced. While Greg was in the medically induced sleep time, Dr. Prusak placed Greg on an antidepressant. I was uncomfortable with this from the start. She assured me that after such a long time in ICU it would be normal for Greg to feel down; she wanted to help with that. She began the medicine while he was sleep induced because it took time to have value. I didn't like the idea and argued mildly, but I wasn't the doctor.

Pam read Scripture to Greg that morning and I prayed. We asked God to please help us make a big step forward. I looked up to see Adele Hanson, from our former church. She came and hugged me and once again the tears came. I was so tired and it blessed me to have someone new come and care. I left her alone with Greg and she sang and ministered by his side. It was very special.

Kim and Lu came later and both told me that they thought Greg looked better. The doctors had told us that even though he was medicated to sleep, that stimulation would be good. Kim and Lu read and sang to him. Joe Kunkel, our neighbor, read Scripture to him. Many offered to spend time with Greg doing whatever they could. Even that was difficult for me – to know what to do. When do you offer stimulation to the patient, and when do you just let him rest? Many, many times the ICU teams assured me that Greg would not remember much of his ICU stay. But while he was there, we wanted to do things right for him. You don't enter into a crisis having just completed a course work on it. You have to face everything with very little information. At those times, I often felt very insecure and uncertain. I am thankful for the many friends and supporters who lent me counsel in those moments.

Later that afternoon, Dr. Poppin, filling in for Dr. Maddy, our kidney specialist, came to me and said that Greg's kidneys looked really good. They were back to functioning so well that the kidney doctors were signing off the case. For the first time in over a week, Greg's temperature was normal. This news brought us a lot of hope.

CHAPTER SIXTEEN

GIFTS AND GRACE

"And my God shall supply all your needs according to His riches in glory in Christ Jesus." Philippians 4:19 NASB

January 24-27

It was now four days since Greg's last surgery, the longest stretch we had had, since entering the hospital, without a surgery. The visitors on the weekends were plentiful. The doctors were allowing Greg more and more time off the ventilator, encouraging his lungs to breathe on their own. I remember thinking constantly, *if he could only get off the ventilator.* We had not been able to speak to Greg with him alert and responding to us in a week. It seemed so long. We missed hearing him speak and we missed the sound of his voice. The girls spent a lot of time caressing their dad's arms and hands and speaking to him. It is a draining thing to spend time with people when it feels like maybe they don't really hear. But the girls hung in there and did whatever they could always trying to stay connected to their dad.

The male nurse on duty that day asked the girls and I how we were doing. Standing across Greg's bed from him I stated that we were getting weary. He immediately pulled us outside of Greg's room and scolded us. He told us we should not say anything negative because Greg could hear us, even though he was asleep. I left the ICU unit in tears. I was not being negative; I was only being honest. I felt it was a bit unfair of him to scold us. I'm sure his intent was probably okay, but I had spent the past 16 days by my husband's side, stressed to the max. I was very weary and had just honestly told him that.

As I went back to the friends in ICU they could see my tears. I told them what had happened, and our friend, John Parr, offered to go into ICU and "take out" that nurse. I thanked him, but said, "probably not a good idea".

Why do I tell about that incident? Mostly because I was learning that there was a real distinction among care professionals. Some of the nurses saw my emotions for what they were, allowed me my grief, understood the burden of the situation and made no judgment as to how we were handling things. Others seemed to want to direct our emotions and us. I don't think anyone can do that. Until you are in the situation, you do not know how you'll be or how you are feeling. We were living moment to moment. We had been hit almost daily with bad news. Even Greg's main physicians were sad and tired. I know I will never judge a person's emotions when someone they love is in crisis. It is best to only be supportive and let them feel what they may.

Greg had breathed on his own without the ventilator for an hour that day. Slowly we were climbing the very steep hill of recovery. Greg's body had so many areas of healing to contend with. I wondered how it had any energy inside of itself. Besides all of the surgical sites to be healed, his body was fighting for lung recovery and against a fever most of the time. On Sunday morning, they showed me pictures of Greg's improving lungs. More and more they were turning off the ventilator, forcing those lungs to work harder and harder. They needed to force the lungs to exercise and take back their responsibility for the body. Greg had a slight fever that morning, but they were not overly concerned. Again, his vitals were strong.

Hurry up and wait seemed to be the order of the day. I remember feeling so anxious to have Greg released from the ventilator. I was also getting anxious to have my husband back home. In our nearly 19 years of marriage we had never been separated that long.

On the home front, our neighbors took care of everything. Each day they made the trip across the lake to let our dog out, check on the house, keep the snow removed, and turn the lights on for when we came home. The Peterson's were wonderful in that way. Teresa always sent food over, leaving us encouraging messages with offers to do anything. I don't know what we would have done without them and the many friends that helped out.

Dave P., as I stated earlier, was there everyday but two. Several years earlier his wife had gone through brain surgery. Hers was successful, in and out, no complications in recovery. But on many levels he fully understood the anxiety and uncertainty of each day. In his own quiet way he watched over me, hovering to meet each need. He actually became my "finance guy" running to the bank for me several times, helping me figure things out. I was so glad he had the time to just spend. We got to know each other pretty well. He brought a certain security for me because I knew each day he would be by.

Pam also was there daily. She would come with phone and message updates from the people she had talked with. I am so grateful she could take on the phone work; I really didn't want to spend the energy or take the time to do that. I know she made some friends by phone!

Food and money kept coming in. It seemed whenever the kids needed something financially, someone had just given me a card with that amount in it. It was perfect. One family gave us a card with $100 worth of gas coupons in it. Talk about a blessing, each time Luke needed gas he would simply grab a coupon. That was such a great idea, especially since we lived out of town and had a fair amount of travel with two cars going back and forth each day.

Greg's former church in Poplar brought us a $150 gift of cash through one of their parishioners. It was so thoughtful of them. Years ago, as a teenager, Greg had mentored their current pastor. Pastor Darrell Nelson spoke highly of Greg's ministry to him. He assured me they would be praying and would do anything else we needed. Their youth pastor, Carey Vik, also came by to visit and support us. Carey had been in Greg's youth group years before and we had both been able to influence Carey to serve in the Poplar church. That they came and shared the burden with me was wonderful. I felt I got to know them both again and it was nice. I know it personally hurt them to see Greg suffering; everyone feared that God might take him from us.

Other friends came with cards and gifts. One in particular that struck me was from John and Sharon Gray. John, too, was from a former church; he and Greg just connected. Mutual respect between two godly men. John really represented for me an elder. Since we were in a new church with a young congregation, the role of elder had not been established. Our pastors came and were wonderful. But John brought something more. He did the work of an elder. As a doctor he fully understood Greg's situation. He helped me to understand it better and to grasp what the journey ahead might be like. He also spoke with great kindness to Greg and prayed over him on more than one occasion. I appreciated them both so much.

One day they placed $40 dollars in a card. Amanda had been shopping with a friend and found a dress she wanted for the Father/Daughter dance in February. It was $40. I told John and Sharon later that they had purchased her dress and blessed her abundantly.

If it had not been for these gifts, I don't know that I would have felt able to indulge the kids. At this point I had no idea what our future would be, financially or otherwise. But through these gifts, our children were able to keep doing the little things that made them feel like they could still live life. Thoughts of their dad were never far away from their minds, but being involved in activities outside of the hospital was a very healthy thing for all the kids.

CHAPTER SEVENTEEN

THE SOUND OF HIS VOICE

"...a time to be silent and a time to speak." Ecclesiastes 3:7b NASB

January 28-30

On Monday, January 28th, our 18th day in the ICU, they were able to remove the ventilator. At 9:15 am they came and told me it had been removed. I had waited for this moment for days. It was a huge victory for us, physically, emotionally, and psychologically. I called the school to get a message to my kids. Immediately, Amanda caught a ride down. She wanted to talk to her DAD! The long week of complete silence was over.

Conversation began. The joy among the family and friends was great. Everyone looked and felt a little brighter, a little lighter and a little stronger. Our hope was being renewed. They were also able to pull Greg's feeding tube. Greg was smiling, interacting, and responding to all of us. My heart overflowed that day with joy. It was the happiest I had felt in a long time.

However, Greg was talking very fast and despite my happiness, I began to feel a little check in my spirit. I tried to dismiss it amongst the happiness that was there. Greg's brother and Mom had come that day and were able to see Greg. It was a great moment for his family. Although they never burdened me with their worries and concerns, I knew how scared they were for their brother and son.

Dr. Fetter had told me the previous Friday or Saturday that he would be out of town for a medical convention. He assured me Greg was in good hands, named the doctors who would be checking on Greg, and said he would see me when he got back. I thanked him for all he had done for us. He told me he didn't usually get involved personally in cases, but that he was involved in this one. He said he was praying, his wife was praying and their church was praying for Greg. What a great man to take the risk to be so involved in our lives. I don't suppose at the time he knew how much we would need him.

Pastor Don Peres came by that day. He himself was working his way back from a stroke and since I had worked as his secretary for years, we had a special bond. It was so good to have him come. I checked on him and he checked on us. It was great to be able to bring him into ICU and have him pray over Greg. And though speech was still something Pastor Don was working on, he prayed beautifully over Greg. I knew Pastor Don understood a lot about our journey and what it takes to walk the road to recovery. He brought me a lot of encouragement that day by his visit.

By the time I got to the hospital on the 29th, Greg was already sitting up and had eaten a small breakfast. The doctors told me that although he had been with a feeding tube, his body was starving and that he needed to eat. Greg felt some dizziness and a little light-headed but seemed to handle it well. After a week of sleeping, he was just glad to be back among the living. I oriented him on the day of the week and month and briefly on the journey he had been through. Now that he was awake, I felt that we could finally look forward with hope that there would be no more bad days.

I continued to have a concern about Greg's constant talking. If people were there, he would chatter rapidly. He had some dreams and some visions in his sleeping state and he talked about them with those who would listen. One such person was his friend Larry Williams. Larry is a great friend and served as our mentor when Greg and I both served in the ministry through Youth For Christ. I know Greg's heart was right and that he had a vision to help Larry's ministry. He was already trying to figure out how God was going to use this, but I kept having this uncomfortable sense. I encouraged Greg that those things could be talked about later and tried to get him to slow down in his discussions. Larry listened patiently to Greg and I think they had a pretty good conversation, but I knew in my heart something was not right.

Since Greg was upright and doing pretty well, I decided to allow two special teens in to see him. Matt Whitaker and John Parr had been to the hospital a lot. Although they weren't playing basketball that year, they had been on the team and under Coach Mirau for the past five. They are good friends of Luke's and the entire family. They were so supportive and caring and I was impressed with how often they came even though they didn't get to see their coach. They were there almost daily and would sit with the girls and I and visit, bringing humor and encouragement. It was refreshing to have them around and I appreciated all the time they gave to us. So on this particular day I thought it would be good for them and for Greg to see each other.

I walked into ICU and told Greg I had some special visitors for him. It was really a magical moment for Matt and John and Greg to see each other. Warm hugs, embracing hand shakes and silent tears were all shared. Greg began his usual "pick-on" John routine and it was wonderful to hear the laughter. Quietly of course as we were still in ICU. We kept the visit short, but as they left John paused, turned around and looked at Greg and said, "Mr. Mirau, to see you again, it's a beautiful thing." "A beautiful thing" is one of Greg's favorite phrases, leave it to John to bring it right back to Greg with all the love and respect in the world.

I did tell the guys not to spread it around at school that they saw Greg. They agreed to keep silent. The hospital had asked us to try to keep visitors to a minimum and we had told the school and several churches that it was best if they didn't come visit. So I didn't need the staff and students thinking it was time to visit. It still wasn't. Many people who came to the hospital never got to see Greg the entire time. But they were great about it as long as they got to connect with the family and receive an update on his condition.

I wonder sometimes how many hundreds of people were praying for Greg. I know it was a lot, only God knows each heart that sought Him on Greg's behalf.

The Petersons (neighbors Brad and Teresa) and Kevin Nordstrom both have little daughters who we love tremendously. They were in the second grade that year and shared a classroom at school. They would daily give each other updates on Greg. It was neat to know how much they cared. We knew they wanted to visit, but Greg's condition was not such that there was a good time for children to come. Plus, we didn't want them scared by seeing all the wires and tubes. He just wasn't the Greg they were used to.

But these two girls separately did a wonderful little thing. In their classroom they were writing a book with other classmates, finishing a sentence of a wish book. While many kids wrote they wished for a horse, or a lot of money, or a new house, or some special toy, Kassie Nordstrom and Hannah Peterson both wrote that they wished "Greg would get well". How special and precious for young ladies to be so unselfish.

Because Greg was awake and Elsie had heard so much about him, I brought her in to meet him. Elsie had gotten to know the girls and I well, and she knew who Luke was, now she could meet their dad. I had told Greg a little about her and her husband and how we had connected in the waiting room. I found Elsie and brought her over to Greg's unit and introduced them and then she took me to John's unit and I met him. Because our medical journeys had begun the same day, and both had taken bad turns, the men could appreciate the relationship we had built.

It was a good connection, I think, for both Elsie and I to visibly see and meet each other's mate. It felt as if it completed the picture of the journey we were both taking with our husbands. I was glad we could share that moment.

On Wednesday, January 30th, we were hopeful that Greg could be moved out of ICU. We had been there 20 days and were extremely weary of ICU, although the nursing staff overall was very kind to us.

This brought on the debate again about where to send Greg. Most heart patients go to 6E for post-cardiac care. But Greg had more concerns. He needed his leg cared for also and that was not the training of the cardiac nurses. It was decided that he still needed to go to 6E and they worked to get him a private room. Greg was so tired. He could not sleep well with the noise and interruptions and just wanted quiet. A private room was arranged for Greg. Because Dr. Fetter was gone, Dr. Maddy did most of the detail work in moving Greg downstairs. Even though he was "off the case", I appreciated that he kept an eye on all of us. Almost daily Dr. Maddy would swing by to check on our family.

Each day new people arrived to greet us, offering prayer and support. It seemed since we had a few days of stability, that we could emotionally start to get a grip on all that happened. There was so much to process. I felt like I had been in the middle of a twister and was finally set down on the ground to assess the damage. But I was still dizzy from all the whirlwinds.

I am so grateful that the initial heart surgery never struggled to heal. Greg's vitals were consistently good. It felt like we were beginning to get around that bend that Clyde had talked about and maybe the straight road was just ahead. We anticipated the move to another floor.

I remember my brother Clyde speaking to me that day and saying, "There's nobody that's been touched by this that hasn't learned something." I suspect that was true; we were all learning something, but I didn't relish that our lives had become the classroom.

In the late afternoon, the decision was made to move Greg to room 6254. Greg had been out of bed twice that day, sitting in his chair. He was eating pretty well and getting used to all that had happened. It took a lot for his body to get used to a vertical position after being on his back so long, but the adjustment was coming.

At 4:30 pm we moved downstairs. They loaded a cart with Greg's growing collection of things including cards and gifts. Matt and John were there visiting so we enlisted their help to carry things. They used the chair Greg was in to wheel him down. The girls and I followed after the nurse and outside of ICU were John and Matt on either side of the hall saluting Coach Mirau as he passed by. It was a cool moment, and I appreciated the respect and humor they brought.

It was decided that the guys would go get a burger for Mr. Mirau. Those kind guys also took my two girls out to eat. Pretty special young men. Matt Whitaker told me later how this whole ordeal had affected him. He said, "It felt like a whole leg or arm had been cut off at school. Mr. Mirau's presence is just so big and all of a sudden it was gone." Many days Matt came to that hospital, his own heart very heavy, yet bringing support to our family. John Parr and he were committed to us. Matt also said that it was so hard to "see someone so strong quickly become so weak." John said, "To so many, Mr. Mirau is larger than life. He had done so much for us, we wanted to do for him". He went on to tell me that their senior year had a lot of challenges. 9/11 had happened that past fall, their friend Pete Newstrom had suffered an injury in football, Geoff Ujdur suffered his injury, Coach Clark's son's illness, and now Mr. Mirau was sick. Coming to see him became "part of the senior routine."

I stayed with Greg while the girls and guys took off. It was nice to have some quiet time before visitors would come by, looking for Greg. This was the first time in 20 days that he wasn't on the 7th floor. I was hopeful that Greg could now enjoy some of the terrific support the kids and I had been receiving. I also wanted people to be able to see him and see for themselves that he was healing.

I ran upstairs to check on Elsie and let her know we had been moved. Her husband would remain in ICU even longer than Greg. Everyone else had come and gone in ICU, but Elsie and I had developed quite a relationship during our long stay. She said she would be down to check on us and I assured her I would stay in touch daily, which I did.

So here we were, on a new floor. It was odd to me how comfortable I had become in my little waiting room corner of the world. Now I didn't have that space and really didn't need it. There was a waiting room just down the hall from Greg's new room where larger groups of people could be. But at this point, we were hopeful to let Greg have company and spend a lot more time with him in his room.

That evening I was visiting with a friend in another part of the building who had stopped by. When we were finished I headed back to Greg's new room. I was amazed to see it full of people. Greg's brother Kirby and his wife, Patti, and family, the Parr's and our girls were all there, along with Dr. Fetter.

He had just come in off the plane and before he went home, had stopped by to check on Greg. He was pleased to see Greg out of ICU. He was busy explaining the journey Greg had been on to the people inside. Although heart surgeons usually do their thing and are out of the patient's life in a few days, he had stuck with us. I listened for a few minutes and then stepped back outside of Greg's room. In a few moments Dr. Fetter joined me. I was so relieved to see him back and gave him a quick impulsive hug. I hadn't realized until that moment how much security he brought to me just with his presence.

He immediately asked me how I was doing. In tears I shared with him my concern that Greg was speaking so much and so rapidly. He told me that he thought he was just happy to be alive. I said that it wasn't like Greg to be so chatty and that I was uncomfortable with how he was. Dr. Fetter noted that he did not know Greg that well, only having met him in the emergency room and took my concerns seriously.

We went back in the room and visited a little more with Greg and the others before they left. We said good night with a promise to be back first thing in the morning. Because the children were doing their best to stay in school and keep up with their studies, I always tried to get them home at a decent time and hoped that they could rest.

Many evenings, alone and quiet, the girls would finally give in to their spent emotions and lay their head on my lap and cry softly. In retrospect, I would still go home every night with my kids. It was the hospital's job to take care of Greg. I knew it was my job to take care of my children. I learned that it was valuable for our family to be together, in our home, even without Greg. Although many families offered us the use of their homes in town, day or night, going to our home each night brought a lot of comfort. It was a mild winter and the roads were not an issue. Maybe if there had been a lot of storms we would have stayed in town.

Even though home brought comfort, the house felt empty and none of us liked it without Greg's bubbly presence. But it did me good to maintain the home. I would do a few chores, keep up with my housework and tend to the children's needs. I believe it helped me stay grounded during that time, and that it kept the shock value in my system from taking completely over. It also helped us to feel that we had a home, a life, a family, and love. Being home in the evenings was a good reminder for us of that truth.

Dr. Fetter had commented to me early on that he noticed I didn't stay at the hospital 24/7 and that I appeared to be taking care of myself. I assured him that I was, or at least I was trying. He was glad to see that I was doing as well as I was and encouraged me to continue to do so.

Since we were moved late in the day, the next morning Greg's nurse, Julie, and the visitor volunteer, Bunny, both came down from the 7th floor to give Greg their best wishes and congratulate him on his move. It was a nice act of kindness. I learned a lot about relationships and the circumstances that can cause them to be developed. Bunny, who had once lived in our neighborhood, we had known, but Julie was new to our lives since the beginning of this journey. I appreciated that Julie cared enough to take the time to follow up with Greg. She had been a great support to me in the early days of our hospital stay. Many times, through tears, I signed release forms for Greg's next surgery, Julie by my side talking me through each one.

CHAPTER EIGHTEEN

SPECIAL VISITORS

"To this end also we pray for you always that our God may count you worthy of your calling, and fulfill every desire for goodness and the work of faith with power." I Thessalonians 1:11 NASB

January 31-February 1

Now that Greg was awake he was missing us more and more. I decided that I would spend the night the up coming Saturday at the hospital with him. He looked forward to it. I didn't really want to spend the night; I was pretty sure I would not get any rest. But I was looking for ways to help Greg heal. I wanted to be sure we were giving him everything he needed for recovery and some extra emotional support would be good.

The leg therapists and rehab doctor came to 6E to see Greg and to do their therapy. It looked as if we were going to begin to have a schedule. Greg had a LP nurse working on his RN who did a lot for Greg and used him as a "case" for his own study. It was nice to have him focus a little more fully on Greg. As he gathered Greg's history, it helped Greg to know more about the journey he was on. He tended to special needs for Greg also, and that was a great act of kindness.

Some of the people who were unable to see Greg in ICU, (doctors who had been shut out) were now able to stop in and say hi in 6E. Daily, Greg had a chance to visit with new people and I think began to get a sense of how widespread his support was. I would often enter his room only to have him introduce me to someone he knew from somewhere, from way long ago. It was truly amazing. A youth who once attended youth groups Greg had led – now a doctor. There were male nurses who stopped in to see Greg who had gone to high school with Greg's brother. Strange, interesting connections like this happened quite a lot. How they even knew Greg was there, I have no idea. But I was encouraged by how well Greg was doing, remembering people and making connections.

Dr. Fetter and I talked about all the people who wanted to see Greg, especially at the school. He understood by now, how loved Mr. Mirau was. He tossed around the idea of giving Greg a "pass" from the hospital and bringing Greg to the school for an assembly. I wasn't sure if it was a good idea, but I did want to bring hope and encouragement to the staff and students at school who were so concerned about Mr. Mirau. If Greg could address the whole student body in a surprise visit, what an encouragement it could be. Dave Parr agreed to speak with the school and look over the logistics of making it happen. The next Monday morning could be a possibility.

Our family practitioner was a little concerned about this idea. She thought it was too much, too soon. She was seeing Greg's struggle to concentrate, his rapid talking, the patterns that did not seem right. As it turned out, it was not going to happen but it would have been fun. In preparation for the possible event I told Greg, "If you go, you need to write down what you are going to say and then say only what you've written down." I was extremely concerned that Greg would not be able to quit talking once he began. He was talking constantly, very, very unlike Greg.

Friday morning the rehabilitation of the leg began. Greg was able to take a slow and careful walk to the door of his room and back. It took an amazing amount of energy, but everyone assured him the leg was strong enough, even with the missing muscle. It was a big moment for Greg to take that first step. With the aid of nurses and the use of a walker, he slowly, meticulously took little steps. His room wasn't large,

126

but to the door and back spent a lot of his strength. It was a good step on the long road of recovery and the goal of going home and complete healing. But he had taken it and was determined.

Since it was a Friday and Greg was doing fairly well, I had decided it might be a good chance for the boys' varsity team to stop by. I made arrangements with Coach Clark for a time that would work and informed the hospital staff of the visit. Everyone was in agreement that this would be fine. They gave us their full support. The Parr family had made a huge amount of cookies, so I brought them along that day for the team to snack on while they visited.

My nephew Matt also came by to see us that day; I don't think he had been there since "Black Thursday," so although Greg was speaking rapidly, he was encouraged to see the progress. The last time he had seen his uncle was at one of Greg's darkest times. Now he was seeing an awake and upright Greg. He did tell me he had never seen his Uncle Greg talk so much.

One thing Dr. Kaylor had asked me to purchase was some high-top shoes for Greg to wear in bed. The high-top laced up would help keep the foot more upright. Well, we found some Chuck Taylor's and Greg was wearing them. Chuck Taylor's were the basketball shoes that Greg wore in high school, so that was kind of funny. Here he was in Chuck Taylor's but definitely not playing ball.

It became the fun idea to have the team sign the shoes when they came. We thought this would help them to make a connection with this coach that had been ill. I'm sure for some of the team, they had never had to visit someone in the hospital. It can be a little frightening. So we tied Greg's shoes on and waited for the team.

I could see the trepidation in the boys' faces as they came in. After all, they had only had updates on Coach Mirau, and most of them hadn't been very good. But as Greg spoke with them, hugged and high-fived them, they relaxed. I think the cookies didn't hurt either. Greg began telling them of defense strategies and soon was talking a mile a minute. I really, really struggled with this constant chatter and mentioned it again to Matt. He didn't know what to make of it either.

One by one, the boys took their turn greeting their loved Coach and signing his shoes, then stepping back enjoyed a cookie. It was a good way for them to connect with Greg, share a moment and break the ice. The shoes now sit on a shelf in Greg's office, a reminder of the day the guys finally were able to see Coach Mirau.

It was wonderful to see the boys make a connection with Coach Mirau, to gain the hope that he would be back with them. Coach Clark had been in to see Greg and I know had passed as many positive messages to them as he could. But maybe seeing is believing and this was an important time for the guys to "see."

Here, too, was an important moment for Luke. He mostly came to the hospital by himself, keeping to his own schedule. But when he was away from us, this team of guys was his support group, encouraging him, keeping him focused and helping in their own way to process. This moment brought those two worlds together for Luke.

Even though it was a special moment, I noticed Greg beginning to repeat himself in what he was telling the guys. As I watched I was inwardly struggling with it. So after about 40 minutes or so, I told them the visit was over, doctors orders, Greg now needed to rest. As the team filed out the door I gave them hugs and thanked them for coming. Many had tears in their eyes. The guys said good-bye and thanked me for the visit. They were to play Denfeld that night so I told them I would see them later.

Neighbors came to see Greg that night and they volunteered to stay with Greg for a while when I went to the game. Always someone was willing to be there. I visited with them in the waiting room on 6E and told them of Greg's constant chatter. I didn't know why he was doing it, but I wanted them to be prepared to spend time with a different Greg. So that night Mark and Brenda Toms and Joe and Linda Kunkel stayed with Greg, reading him scripture, but mostly listening to him chatter. I found I needed a break from the constant talking. They all experienced a very different Greg from the one they knew. Brenda said later to Greg teasingly, "You would not shut up Greg! I'm a talker and even I could not out-talk you." Mark, her husband, told us one evening much later, "I watched Greg struggle with words and be so chatty, I worried he would not be able to read the Christmas story to us." We have an annual neighborhood Christmas party each year and Greg's tradition is to read the story from the Bible. Mark and Brenda were both blessed to hear him read those words beautifully that next Christmas.

Dick Bloomquist, a friend from Salem Covenant, had come by that day too. I let him see Greg briefly (Greg had seen a lot of company already), and then we went to visit in the waiting room. He handed me a card from Salem, encouraging me to open it. Inside was $500 from his church. He said they wanted to show their love in a tangible way. In tears I thanked him. Greg had served that church as youth pastor 18 years ago. We were married in that church, but had not attended there in years having moved to a different neighborhood. What an act of compassion from that body of believers. Again, I was overwhelmed.

Later that evening I found myself in the gymnasium of Denfeld High School. A dad and grandpa of one of the players, Justin, stopped me and asked about Greg. I gave them an update and then I said, "These boys are going to state this year." They looked at me sort of surprised and with a little bit of doubt.

The team had struggled so much with their game while Greg was ill. They and I knew the team was not playing very well. I shared with them the story of my brother Dan. After many battles with his heart, and finally by-pass surgery, his son's football team had gone to state for the 1st time in their school history. I had celebrated a lot in my heart for my brother Dan, his wife, Candy, and those boys. He could have easily missed watching his sons play football in the Metrodome, but he had been here. In my heart I knew this was going to be Marshall's destiny also. Well, maybe not the Metrodome, but definitely a trip to state.

I repeated myself saying these boys are going to state this year, and Greg will be there to watch them. I'm not sure where that confidence came from, or if I just really, really wanted something good for those boys. They looked at me with a bit of disbelief, but hoped that I was right.

The team lost their game that night. I was a little discouraged. I asked Coach Clark if maybe it was too much emotionally for them to see Greg as he was. He told me no. If anything, seeing Greg was just what the team needed. After all, those boys had waited to see the coach for 21 days, a long time of wondering if they would ever see him again. Coach Clark felt nothing but positive about the team's visit and I decided that I needed to trust him about that. These were amazing young men, and I still believed something good was going to happen.

CHAPTER NINETEEN

SEIZING----THE MOMENT!

"I was brought low, and He saved me." Psalms 116:6b NASB

February 2-3

The next day was Saturday, the night I had decided I would spend with Greg at the hospital. He was feeling more and more lonely and the kids said they would be fine at home without me. Because of the decision to stay all night, Kevin encouraged me to sleep in and spend the morning at home. I had not had a morning at home in 21 days. He planned to be at the hospital early that day and would keep Greg company.

So that is what we did. About 9:30 am or so I received a call from Dr. Prusak. She noted that Dr. Fetter had cancelled the prozac dose for Greg. I told her I was comfortable with that. She was not; she felt that Greg's rapid talk and inability to focus as he should would be helped by the prozac. I felt that the prozac was maybe part of the problem causing the rapid talk. She wanted to put him back on the dosage. I again said I didn't really want to do that. I felt that Greg did not really need the "support" of extra medicine. She got me to reluctantly agree to a half-dose of the prozac. I asked her to look for Kevin and inform him of her decision. I suppose she didn't quite understand why I would ask her to do that, but in my book, Kevin had as much authority about Greg as I did. If any more questions should be asked, I had complete confidence that Kevin would ask them.

I arrived at the hospital around noon with the girls. Greg seemed a little more peaceful that day, a bit more relaxed. But he still wasn't sleeping well. I had such high hopes that he could get good rest on the 6th floor, being quieter than the

131

ICU. It wasn't happening like I had hoped. We all agreed that we needed to keep people out and to limit the stimulation. Maybe he just had too much company. He had his physical therapy and then I left his room for him to nap. Of course, he had a phone call, which he took and he never really did rest. He was so sleep deprived. I guess this is a common occurrence for hospital patients. As hard as I tried to get him to sleep, sleep just didn't come. He could not relax. He knew he was very tired, but rest eluded him.

Luke picked the girls up that evening, checking on his dad and heading home with his sisters. I prepared to spend the evening with Greg. The next day was Superbowl Sunday and the Lucas family was bringing dinner. We had found a room at the other end of the hospital where we could watch the game together. It promised to be a good day for all of us, and I was especially hopeful for Greg. I thought this would help him see the progress he was making and give him endurance for the days ahead.

Luke and the girls promised to be back in the morning. I crawled alongside Greg on his bed, holding him and comforting him. He had a lot of scars that were healing, so I worked carefully to not bump anything. About 11:00 pm we tried to settle down and rest. I wasn't very comfortable in my chair, but I was hoping if I stayed, Greg would feel safe and then sleep better. He did doze and sleep a little, but not a lot. There are so many hospital noises and interruptions. I could not sleep, but listened carefully to my husband's breathing and the beeping of the monitors. We had tried everything we knew to keep Greg comfortable. He had ear plugs and a sleeping mask for his eyes. Even with all this, he slept very poorly. Although sleep eluded us, I took comfort in knowing I was there with my husband, and my husband was still here with me.

Early in the morning I got up from my makeshift bed, freshened up and prepared for the day. Greg took a walk to the waiting room and we sat in there for quite a while. Another patient came in and he and Greg visited. But once Greg began to talk, it was if he could not stop. I felt so sorry for that man. He received more information about Greg than he wanted. But he was gracious and listened well.

Greg had asked me to get him a new bathrobe. Again, I was noting a change in Greg. He was struggling so much to get the words out as he tried to describe the kind of bathrobe I should get him. What was causing this? Instead of his speech getting better and slowing down, Greg was stuttering and losing ability to focus on conversation. Finally by his pointing to the blue chair, I knew he wanted a blue bathrobe. The more Greg struggled to find words and gather thoughts, the more anxious I was feeling inside. What was making him do this? Why did Greg just not seem like himself?

When the stuttering started to happen I became increasingly concerned. This was something Greg has never done. Mixed-up thoughts, difficulty finding words, rapid chatter, repeating himself. It took so much patience to try and decipher what he was saying. I found that inside, I just wanted to run away. I didn't know how to handle this. I discussed it with a few friends, but none of us seemed to have any answers.

I decided I would also take Abbey shopping that afternoon and get her an outfit for the upcoming father/daughter dance while I found a robe for Greg. Kevin said he would stay with Greg. I shared with him my concerns over Greg and together we decided to continue to limit visitors that day. Maybe it was that Greg was getting too much stimulation. I knew with Kevin watching the door, Greg's room would remain quiet. The nurses also posted a notice on the door, requesting visitors to check with them before entering.

Kevin shared my concerns about Greg, but he didn't have any answers either. We were all trusting that the doctors knew what was happening. Maybe in post-op recovery this is what happens. I know I felt totally confused by this condition, and began to feel I did not know my husband any longer. It was an awful feeling.

Chico, the religion teacher from Marshall, came by that day. Although he had been by to see me, this was the first time he was able to see Greg. Kevin wasn't going to let him in, but I said I wanted him to. Chico brought warm wishes and support to Greg. He spoke encouraging words and brought loving thoughts from the school.

He told Greg that his wife, meaning me, was a "theophany" for him, the presence of God in his room. (I made sure Kevin heard that!) Later Karen Snyder came by for a visit and it was decided she would sit with Greg while we went to lunch. She, too, knew that Greg wasn't himself. None of us knew what to do about it. So now I had a lunch break and a break coming via a shopping trip with my daughter. I loved Greg so much, but this different Greg was making me weary.

After I came back from shopping, Greg got in his new robe and perched up on the bed. He was looking forward to the Superbowl party. We had spent many Superbowls with the Lucas' family. This time because Greg was at the hospital, we had agreed to have a party at the hospital. We had secured a quiet waiting room where we could just be us. Scott and Meg organized everything in the room we had set aside. Before the game, Scott and Kevin were in with Greg. He was still talking rapidly, but they were encouraged to just have time with Greg. As game time approached, the kids and the Lucas family headed down to our designated space. I wanted so much for Greg to slow down, enjoy some time with family and friends, and to have a sense of relief from the daily strain.

I was exhausted but kept trying to stay upbeat, fighting my feelings of insecurity concerning Greg's speech issues.

Kevin and I went to get Greg's wheelchair outside of his room, but it was gone. Dr. Fetter had found us a special chair that would meet Greg's needs with his leg. Because it was no longer outside the room we headed down the hall to find another. We found one a ways away and headed back to Greg's room. I casually opened the door to Greg's room, ready to load him up.

What I found was terrifying. As I opened Greg's door I knew immediately that Greg was having a seizure. My husband's body was totally stiff and shaking on the bed. I screamed to Kevin who rushed to Greg's side, holding him on the bed. He told me to get the nurse and I pushed the button and went running out of the room to find the nearest nurse. I told her my husband was seizing, and she asked me "What?" I said, "My husband is having a seizure!" She looked in on Greg's room and saw Kevin holding Greg on the bed. He told her the same thing, "He's having a seizure!" She ran to the nurses station, and soon "Dr. Heart" was quickly announced over the intercom.

Within a matter of minutes, doctors, nurses, and technicians with equipment were racing into Greg's room. Kevin and I stepped outside of the room as a hoard of people hovered around his bed. I remember saying to Kevin, "What's happening, I can't take another something going wrong." He didn't know, but assured me that they were there and that he would be taken care of.

I heard the doctor say, "He's coming out of it", and then she began to talk to Greg, asking him if he could hear her, focus on her, other such questions. I decided to head down towards the waiting room, unsure of what I would tell my children. We had finally had a celebration planned, and now this. As I rounded the bend to the other section of hospital, I saw Scott heading toward me. I flung myself into his arms and told him weepingly that Greg had had a seizure. I could not answer any other questions. Scott had heard the "Dr. Heart" and told Meg he was going to wander back towards our way. After all, they were wondering why we hadn't shown up with Greg.

He walked with me back to Greg's area and Kevin told us they were still looking at Greg. Nurses and technicians and other people entered and left; Greg's room was like a revolving door. I called Pam and asked her to come to the hospital. Scott headed back to the party room to talk with our children and his own. Before long, the girls and Luke were in my arms, the girls crying so hard. The fear that came upon us at that moment was so huge. I remember feeling that it wanted to overpower me, but I could not let it with my children right there.

Pam showed up quickly and Abbey went to her immediately. Kevin guarded over Amanda. Our friend Joe Kunkel had come by that evening to just check on us, so he had his arm around me. Luke was with his friend Matt. We were all taken care of. Inside Greg's room the doctors and nurses were still hovering. I'm sure they thought he was having heart issues and they were watching closely.

Luke called Coach Clark and told him that his dad had had a seizure. Before many minutes went by, Greg began to seize again. Once again "Dr. Heart" was called and the staff came flying.

The girls were peering into their dad's room and saw their dad's legs go stiff. The weeping was intense. Abbey and Amanda were crying so hard. Luke looked like he was stunned. How were my kids going to survive this? Was this the end for Greg? How much more could his body endure, what damage could be done to new surgeries only beginning to heal?

Amanda had called Pastor Ryan a few minutes before. Pastor was a great security for the kids and told them to call him anytime for any reason. Well, Amanda had a reason and she needed him. As I was sitting there outside Greg's room, waiting for answers, Pastor Ryan came flying down the hall toward us, Bible in one hand, jacket draped and flying over the other shoulder. I remember thinking, this is like a bad movie. Is any of this even real? I mean Pastor was really moving, ready to be there for us, no matter what. It was all so surreal. We were traumatized, totally frightened, not knowing what to hold on to or what to believe. It seemed that everything stopped for a moment and I still have in my mind the full picture of that scene as if it were on a big movie screen.

As Pastor Ryan was coming to the hospital, he had called a group of college students he knew were having a Superbowl party and told them they needed to pray for Greg. He heard a student speaking there, "Shut off the TV, we need to pray." Those college kids, many who did not know us, hit that remote and went to prayer on our behalf totally unconcerned about the Superbowl.

I went to find Elsie. It seemed whenever there was a change, I needed Elsie to know, and I hope she felt the same with us. After all, we had begun these terrible journeys on the same day. They were still in our familiar waiting area upstairs and I told them briefly what was happening. They came down to be with us, embracing our hurts and sharing the burden with us. I will forever treasure the special relationship we were able to form with them. It was a comfort to have Elsie by my side; we had been through so many tough times together.

We gave Ryan the update of the little we knew, and he prayed immediately. Here were all these men around, each about as scared as I, offering strength, love, prayer, and support, each need being met, even though I didn't know what I needed. Greg's friend Jim Rich also came by. I know he was hoping for some good news. I felt badly when we had to share with him the frightening turn of events that had just occurred. He left saying he would be praying for all of us, his shoulders sagging a little more.

The doctor came out and assured us that it was not related to Greg's heart. His vitals were still stable. They were going to take him for a CAT scan and we could go in and see Greg for a few minutes. Of course, we all had tears in our eyes, right when we wanted to be strongest for him.

Kevin explained to Greg what had happened. Someone prayed over him. We assured Greg of our love. I think Joe read scripture. The girls, Pam and I all gave him a little kiss on the cheek. I know in his own way, Greg was trying to comfort and assure us, but of course he did not really know what was happening to his own body. In a few moments the aids came to get Greg for his CAT scan and the nurses directed us back up to ICU.

Greg said later he knew something was wrong when Scott Lucas was standing over his bed and looking at him when the Superbowl was on! Scott loves football and especially the Superbowl! It always amazed me how much Greg fought and worked to keep his mind focused on what was happening. He said later he knew he was having the second seizure because he could feel his body tensing up but was helpless to do anything about it.

I know within myself that I was totally spent. Sometimes I don't even know how you breathe when you feel such fear, but you do. You dig deep at those times and I pulled myself together, sort of. We did not have any answers, and in that moment there were a thousand questions.

We loaded Greg's items onto a cart; somehow we knew he would not be back in that room again. I never liked being on the 6th floor. The whole week we were there, Greg never seemed like himself. He was making physical progress, but it seemed we were losing mentally. The night of the seizures seemed to culminate that truth.

Luke went to the Lucas' home with Matt and his siblings. He did better not having to be in the middle of it. There was a part of me that thought at times Luke should have stayed with me. But I needed to let Luke make his own decisions and leaving seemed to help Luke cope. I knew Luke was well taken care of at the Lucas home.

We sat in the ICU waiting room for quite a long time and just didn't hear anything. I finally went to medical ICU, asking if Greg was there. They said yes and that I could come in. This was a new ICU unit for us. I was directed to the end unit where Greg was. He had been sedated and was fast asleep, again hooked up to all kinds of machines. I wondered, "Will he have another seizure? What caused this one? Where do we go from here?"

The neurologist on call was at the nurse's desk. I went over to him and asked if they had found anything. He said the initial tests showed the brain was fine, they had placed Greg on anti-seizure medicine and that for now they would just let him rest. He did not have any answers for me. From all initial tests Greg's body was again stable. He would be watched closely during the night.

I went back to family and friends waiting for me, told them what I knew, which was nothing, and sat down for a moment. Before I knew it, Coach Clark, Coach Radzak and Coach Newstrom were coming down the hall. Kevin had seen Coach Newstrom outside the waiting room and said he was white as a ghost. He told Bob that Greg's vitals were stable. Coach Clark came to me immediately and embraced me in a big hug. I apologized for crying, telling him I was just so tired.

Unbeknownst to me, another patient on the 6th floor with a room next to Greg had a connection to Coach Clark and had called him believing that Greg had died. All three coaches drove to the hospital because they thought they had lost their friend that night. Kevin had told Bob that Greg was stable, but Bob had not been able to speak to Coach Clark. So while Bob and Coach Radzak knew that Greg had not died, Coach Clark did not. Coach Clark thought it was strange for me to apologize for crying; after all, in his mind I had just lost my husband. He stood there holding me, trying to think of what to say to me, believing that I had just become a widow. While we stood there, Coach Radzak leaned forward and whispered in his ear, "He didn't die."

The trauma those men must have felt and the compassion they came with for the children and I was astounding. I cannot express what it meant, and I cannot understand how they felt. It was a horrible, terrible, wonderful night. To go from deep, deep grief, to still some hope in a matter of minutes. I am sure in those moments the weight of the world rested on their shoulders. They did not tell me that night what they had thought; it was two days later before I would know the traumatic feelings they had gone through. They are terrific men and I love and respect them all.

Pastor Ryan gathered us in a circle of prayer in that ICU waiting room that night. Here were my close friends, the coaches, my daughters and I, gathered and praying, focused on one man. It was a powerful moment that I shall never forget.

I took Coach Clark, Kevin, and the girls in to see Greg. I felt it was important for Coach Clark to see Greg still breathing, still hanging in there, so that he could alleviate the fears of the team the next day. The girls of course needed that same assurance. Kevin I brought along for me. It helped me on many occasions to have Kevin see Greg because he could then later assure me that Greg really was okay. Pastor

Ryan, the coaches, and Kevin brought me so much reassurance and comfort.

Even though we could not speak to Greg, it did all of our hearts good to see him. He was lying there, resting, like nothing had happened at all. The beeping of the monitors, the steady up and down movement of his chest, the restful look on his face, all made us feel a little more safe. We headed for home, traumatized again, but grateful we too were still breathing.

It meant phone calls to family and others to update them on the day's events. Our special party day had gone very badly. None of us saw the Superbowl that night. None of us cared.

CHAPTER TWENTY

NEW HOPE?

"The light is pleasant, and it is good for the eyes to see the sun."
Ecclesiastes 11:7 NASB

February 4-5

On Monday, February 4th, I headed for the hospital very tired from the previous evening. I had not slept well with the images of my seizing husband fresh in my mind. I was hoping for some answers to yesterday's questions. A call to the hospital before I left home assured me Greg had been stable through the night. The girls came to the hospital with me; they could not have focused on school that day anyway. We were all anxious for answers.

We headed into the ICU to see Greg alert and eating breakfast. We recounted with him what had happened the previous evening. Greg looked at us and said, "I bet you were scared." The understatement of the day! There were no doctors around at that time so I was not finding any answers very fast. We were all grateful to see him looking well and he was feeling pretty good. It was almost as if it had not happened, but it had. In some ways Greg seemed more like himself that morning than he had on any previous day. A bouquet of balloons and a card with money had arrived, a gift from Mark and Brenda, our neighbors. We read the kind, encouraging note, always grateful for the support that arrived on a daily basis.

I headed down the hall to get a cup of coffee when Dr. Eckman came toward me. He stopped me and said, "Robynne, I'm so sorry. I heard about Greg's seizures. It was the antibiotic we were giving him. It's a very strong antibiotic, and one of the side effects is seizures." They were trying so hard and tenaciously to fight any infections and had upgraded his dose. It was too much and Greg's body could not tolerate anymore, thus the seizures. I have always appreciated how Dr. Eckman handled that with me. Upfront and honest. At least now I knew the cause. They would keep Greg on an anti-seizure medication for a while; they had to be certain it would not happen again and it would take a while for the medication already given to diminish from his body.

Greg was in remarkable good spirits; the seizures didn't affect him adversely. Many told me later that seizures are much more frightening than they are harmful. On the morning that we had hoped Greg could make a surprise visit to the Marshall School, we found ourselves back in ICU, only this time the Medical Intensive Care Unit.

The MICU unit is somewhat different from the SICU. In the hallway, SICU nurses asked me what we were doing back there on the 7th floor, and I told them briefly. Hospital policies do not allow the nurses to enter any other ICU unit but where they work, so they sent their best wishes to Greg through us.

Larry Williams came by that day and went in to see Greg. I had asked him to keep it short because Greg became tired. He agreed. I also wanted Larry to "take charge" because Greg was still chatting a lot. After quite a long while I went in to get Larry who had been trying to leave. I had to tell Greg, somewhat firmly, that Larry needed to leave now. After we got out of there, Larry told me he just couldn't get away. He had tried several times, but Greg would not stop talking. I knew what he meant. That constant need to chatter did not seem to be getting any better. In the back of my mind it was really annoying me.

On Tuesday, February 5th, we received some news that made us feel we were finally going to make progress. There had been no more seizures and word was that they would transfer Greg over to the rehab hospital for therapy. Dr. Fetter had told us that they would love Greg there because he was so "re-habitable". I was relieved that we didn't have to go back to 6th floor; our experience there had not been positive. I felt no connection to the staff there and it had been a hard week. Maybe a new hospital would bring some much needed progress.

In the ICU unit that Greg was in there was a big concave mirror on the upper right corner. From there the nurses could see Greg, and he could see people coming in. As time progressed, Greg watched that mirror more and more. Clyde picked up on how much Greg would watch that mirror, almost obsessed with watching it. Greg's mom and brother came that day to check on him. Grandma and Clyde thought he looked a lot better. He was better but still talking so very much. And now, as I look back, I realize he was beginning to become a little obsessive. Something was still not right.

At one point on Tuesday morning I was going to check on Abbey, whom I thought was with her dad. She was just outside of the MICU unit visiting and comforting another lady. It seemed this person's father was dying in the unit next to Greg. He had some kind of disease and because of the pain he was in, they could not touch him. Abbey had apparently seen her crying and tried to comfort her. She had told her that her dad was in there too. I was struck by the strength in my young daughter to stop and bring comfort to someone quite a bit older. I think that lady was impressed too. Another poignant moment on our journey.

By mid-afternoon we were ready to roll. They brought the lift team in, had Greg situated in a wheelchair, a cart full of goodies rolling behind. It was like a parade with so many of us following the nurse with Greg, someone pushing the cart and our arms loaded with items. Dave P. carried the balloons making it feel like a real party.

On the skywalk over, Greg could finally get a real look at the outside world. He enjoyed seeing the traffic, the sunshine, and the people walking in the skywalk. This was fun for him, to finally feel some freedom. He greeted the people as we walked by.

I was hopeful that real therapy would take place here and we would soon be able to take Greg home. The room we were brought to was bigger and brighter than any he had been in. He was the only patient in there, for the moment, and we were hoping to keep it a private room. Across the floor was another family we had met during our journey whose son was now in therapy. They too were anxious to be home. I chatted with his parents briefly inquiring as to how their son's progress was coming.

Of course in our excitement we failed to let everyone know of our transition. Scott Lucas and Kevin N. did eventually find us that evening and shared in our joy that we had crossed another bridge. Now Scott could make a quick jaunt and find us after work, as we were much closer to his office.

It was very hard to leave Greg in that new hospital that evening. The nurse's desk was so far away, the room was big, and I felt bad leaving him there. It seemed like it would be a much more lonely place, and I struggled with that. Greg's brother and nephew stopped by that afternoon as well as my friend Robin. Greg was talking with his brother, Kirby, about plans for summer work and asking Kirby to do some things. I shook my head no at Kirby, indicating to him to not carry out any of Greg's requests. Somehow I knew that Greg was getting way ahead of himself and that the thinking process was not what it was supposed to be. But while Kirby was with Greg, Robin and I had a chance to take a walk and catch up in another part of the hospital.

In his new room we were hopeful that Greg would be able to get some good rest. I could tell that he was extremely tired. He was still speaking rapidly and he greeted everyone in the hall. Was he really just happy to be alive? The uneasiness in my heart grew. I never loved it when Greg was too quiet and wouldn't talk to me, but this constant chatter was not making me any happier.

CHAPTER TWENTY-ONE

A NEW BATTLE

"Where then does wisdom come from? And where is the place of understanding?" Job 28:20 NASB

February 6-7

On Wednesday morning, they showed me Greg's therapy schedule. He was to have physical therapy concentrating on the leg and some occupational therapy and other skills worked on. As the day progressed, I felt lost. I did not know the staff here. Greg now had a new doctor for rehab and the people who I had become so familiar with were not in the picture anymore. For the past three weeks I had seen the same doctors who gave me morning updates. Dr. Fetter, Dr. Eckman, Dr. Maddy, Dr. Kaylor and Dr. Prusak would find me daily and inquire about how we were, give me their positive comments on Greg and just be a general encouragement. They had "passed us on" to a new care group and rightfully so. But I missed the security I had developed in them always being there. Dr. Prusak did come by and see Greg at the rehab hospital, but we just did not cross paths there. Everything was different now. If I was feeling so disoriented, I wondered how Greg was.

The social worker came by, the psychotherapist, the physical therapist, the occupational therapist, the nurse for the moment, and the doctor. So many new people so quickly, all asking a lot of questions, trying to do their jobs. It seemed that they didn't thoroughly look at Greg's medical chart because many were surprised when we said Greg's leg was the side issue. They didn't realize the amazing heart surgery he had survived. I suppose in Greg's medical records it was many, many pages back.

As the day progressed instead of things becoming easier, they became more difficult. My brother-in-law called that morning and was so excited that we had made the move. We should have been able to celebrate that fact. But I had to put him off saying things weren't all that good yet and that I would explain later, which I did.

Greg's speech became more and more rapid. The stuttering elevated also. Dave P. spent some time in Greg's room that morning and saw the same thing. When Greg would be taken to therapy we would try to analyze what was going on with Greg. I spoke with the psychotherapist at her request. She was concerned about his speech issues and concentration struggles. I told her I thought it was related to the medication, that this was not how my husband usually acted. She made a note and we ended our conversation.

A compulsiveness, which I had never seen in Greg before, seemed to emerge from nowhere. He became demanding, wanting everything in order. He had us repeatedly cover his feet, over and over again, because the sheets or blankets weren't just right. Who was this person? Kevin recalls spending 3 hours on that Wednesday evening just adjusting sheets and blankets to get them right. This was not the Greg we knew. Although he was demanding, he was not unkind. He would patiently explain to any of us what he thought needed to be done to adjust a pillow, or blanket or whatever he was concerned about at that moment. It was just so strange to see him behave like that.

When the girls came that afternoon, Amanda became a servant to her dad, trying to please him and help him. The psychotherapist who had met with Greg and saw his concentration issues told him he needed to look people right in the eye and that they needed to do that back. She told him and me that this would help him with his concentration. This became demanded by Greg and not an option. In Greg's own way he was trying to do everything that the medical staff asked of him because he wanted to go home. But in his altered mental state he could not see the obsessive person he was becoming. If we would even blink away, he would become frustrated with us. It made me, and others, not even want to be there. Greg generally doesn't watch much TV but now he began to obsess on it. He would obsess on the position of his pillows or the way the tray sat on the stand. Just about everything.

Greg's nurse that afternoon was a guy named Kurt. He introduced himself and asked us about Greg's journey. As I was explaining what had happened, Greg asked us to leave the room; he did not want to hear our conversation. We stepped outside and I gave him a brief rundown although it was hard to be brief when our journey had become so complicated. But in that conversation I was able to share my concerns about Greg's mental state. He assured me he would keep a close eye on him and I did feel that Kurt really heard me. I still wasn't convinced that Greg would not have another seizure or some other complication.

One of the basketball parents, Mike Machones, came by that day. I let him see Greg, but warned him that Greg was not himself. Mike was gracious and made a good visit out of it. I think he, too, could see that there was something wrong. Mike's son and a basketball player, Adam, had made a wonderful cover for a blank autograph book for Greg. It had been passed around at a basketball game and then left at the hospital for people to sign.

The cover Adam made really stated Greg's, Coach Mirau's role in the lives of the team and the school. It says:

Mirau, Dad, Coach, Teacher, Friend, The Big Guy

The autographs inside are heart-warming, wonderful compliments to my husband, their teacher and coach. I look back on them and have realized even more, the gift of love that Greg bestows on people. Each note is laced with thanks, respect and admiration for this beloved coach.

Adam Machones was in 9th grade the year Greg became ill, yet he was a starter for the basketball team. He and Luke have remained good friends for the past three years and always connect when Luke is home from school. Adam sat down and shared his thoughts about Coach Mirau's journey and the team's journey that year.

"When I first heard that the Big Guy was in the hospital with a heart problem I did not know the severity of the situation. I thought that he would be there for a night or miss one day of school or something. I expected him to be back at practice right away. He seemed to be invincible to me before this whole situation. When I finally heard the whole story and the state that the Big Guy was in, I felt terrible. First I felt guilty for not knowing how severe it was. Then I felt just terrible for him and his family. I remember thinking that Mr. Mirau was the one man on the earth that was the least deserving of what happened to him. But when it was all over, I thought that he handled his situation better than anyone on earth could have. When he was in the hospital, I remember before the Denfeld game, we all went down to visit him. I showed up with Aaron Sillanpa. We were one of the first ones there. We walked into his room and his eyes were closed and his tongue was hanging out of his mouth. We were both stunned and kind of stood there wondering what we should do. Then a huge smile came across Mr. Mirau's face. He started laughing. We were amazed at this great attitude. He pulled the same 'tongue hanging out' trick for everyone that day when they entered.

"When everyone got there, he said a prayer for us. He was done in about 60 seconds, but then he rambled on and on, all excited about our game that night. He told us the difference between average players and great players, good teams and great teams. He told us everything about the game of basketball. "

As I looked at that notebook sitting in Greg's room and thought about all the kind messages from the team and others, I knew even more strongly that we had to fight against this mental battle that was raging in Greg. We had to get him back fully. But how? I had no idea what I was even fighting.

By the end of the day I had had it. I spoke with Pam, Kevin, Dave P., and Scott L., all people who knew Greg well. We unprofessionally agreed that it must be the medications. I determined the next day I would be there early and find his rehab doctor. Something had to be done!

With Kevin and Scott's support, I wrote a note and left it for the rehab doctor requesting that Greg be pulled off the prozac medication. My professional friends who knew Greg well stated that they believed he did not need that medicine. I had the nurses tape it to the front of Greg's chart with an insistence that they make sure the doctor received my note. Prozac was not the only problem with Greg, but it was the one medication that I knew wasn't life-saving for Greg, and it was a place I could start in helping him get back to normal. Dr. Prusak told me later she did see my note to the rehab doctor and did not challenge my request. I appreciate her respect in that moment.

The next morning I was at the hospital by 7:00 am. I checked in at the nurse's station and asked if the rehab doctor was in. They said not yet. I asked them to please make a note to him that I wished to speak with him.

I waited in Greg's room and I wandered the halls looking for the doctor. I knew that a conversation with him was imperative. Greg had not slept well again, was struggling with concentration, speaking rapidly, seeming agitated. I was increasingly frustrated. Even the stuttering seemed to increase. As much as I wanted to love and support Greg, it became increasingly difficult to spend any amount of time with him. He was just so not like himself.

The routine of therapy continued, the therapists doing their job, despite Greg's mental struggle. I realize now that they just didn't really pay attention to it. Maybe on some level the program is too specialized, or maybe our doctor just wasn't seeing the whole picture.

By about 10:00 am I was able to have my meeting with the doctor. Greg was down in therapy and we sat in Greg's room. The rehab doctor seemed very uncomfortable with me, a little nervous, but maybe that was his nature.

I told him of my concerns, documenting everything I could think of. I told him Greg's speech was too fast, that he was stuttering, he could not seem to sleep well, and that he was becoming obsessive in some of his behavior. The doctor basically blew me off, telling me that because of Greg's long stay in the hospital he probably had "Hospitalitis" and just needed to go home. He told me he had seen my note concerning the prozac and that at my insistence, the medication had been pulled.

He offered me little assurance or comfort concerning Greg. I don't know if he just could not see it, would not believe it, or what was wrong. But in all of our time at the hospital, I had never felt so uncared for. It seemed that the only support I had at that hospital was Kurt, our male nurse. And I think as he worked with and watched Greg, he could see what we were seeing. I am grateful that at least one person could hear us there.

Greg was still on another strong antibiotic. That day I asked Dr. Eckman's fill-in if he needed to remain on the medications. She, too, was a former Marshall parent and listened well when I told her of Greg's strange behavior. Because Greg's lungs were now healthy, and the fever was gone, she felt that he could be removed from the antibiotic. Maybe we were making progress. Two less medications he had to be on.

In the meantime, Greg had been given a roommate, an older man who had been through some type of head surgery. In Greg's obsessive state, he became overly concerned for the roommate who was struggling. On some levels I could not blame Greg for paying attention to his roommate. At one point the man tried to get out of his wheelchair and into bed by himself. He nearly fell on the floor as I raced to get a nurse. His understanding of his status was not clear and he would attempt to do what he could not. For all of us this became a concern but not something Greg needed to take on. Just more stress.

Seeing that happen made me more uncomfortable with Greg's situation there. His room was a long way from the nurse's desk, and I felt that it would be easy for them not to pay attention. In the back of my mind was that frightening night of seizures. I still felt that at any minute something could go wrong.

As the day wore on, so did the tension. In the afternoon, Greg came back from a therapy session where he was to make a tuna-fish sandwich. Because he could not find the mayonnaise jar, the therapist became impatient with him. When he tried to clean up the counter, she was frustrated. How was he supposed to know that he was to use the mayo packs or that she didn't care about the counter being clean? For Greg, that was how he would do things at home.

Greg was trying his best to keep control in his head, to please the therapists, and to do things right. To have to practice making a sandwich in his situation seemed

155

demeaning. Then added onto that was the mental stress his brain was obviously under. She apparently scolded him. By the time he was returned to his room, he was minutes from an emotional breakdown.

In my arms, that is what happened. Greg sobbed. He explained to me in his confused state how she treated him, how humiliated he felt, that no one respected him as a man, as the owner of his own business, as a teacher, or as a coach. He felt he was treated as a dummy. This hospital where Greg was supposed to get the utmost care and make steady progress was contributing to his emotional destruction. I was furious, but didn't know where to turn.

Greg cried and I handed him tissues, hugging and assuring him that I loved him, all the while trying to really understand what he had been through. He would use the tissues and then refold them neatly and hand them back to me - more of the obsessive-compulsive behavior. Greg's head was clearly out of control, but where do you get help when no one really seems to believe you?

We were about a half an hour away from the kids coming from school to visit their dad. I asked Greg if he felt he could see them and if he could stop crying. He wanted to see them, and I watched as he pulled all the wherewithal he could to bring it together for his children.

The girls and Luke came by; Luke for a brief visit before basketball practice. With all the strength he could muster, Greg asked the kids about the day, caught up with Luke on basketball stuff and loved on his kids.

As evening came Greg was more fatigued. He had not slept at all that day and he became more and more compulsive. Dave and Diane Parr came and my sister Barb. Kevin and Scott L. came after their workday. We watched in dread as Greg's mental state deteriorated. We took him in his wheelchair to a waiting area to try to visit and had his supper brought there. Over and over again, he would have Amanda arrange his blanket over his leg. Wrapping and re-wrapping his legs. As soon as she would do exactly as he asked, he would decide that he wanted it a little bit different.

I remember Scott L. saying it broke his heart to watch Amanda try to please her dad. I will say this, Amanda had the patience of Job that day, and over and again would listen to what her dad wanted. Of course, Greg had no idea what he was really doing and Amanda never tired of trying to please him. All of our goals were to get Greg home.

Because the Parr's and my sister Barb were going to stay a little later, I decided to go home with the girls. I was so tired from that day and from trying to reason with people about Greg's condition. It was a real release to leave him for a while, but of course I had mixed feelings of abandoning him in crisis. Still I knew he was in excellent care with my sister and the Parr's there.

John Parr and Matt Whitaker had come that evening too, running down from the Marshall School. I thought they were maybe a little crazy, knowing that the run back was all uphill. It was nice to see them again, but they were not able to see Greg that night.

Kevin walked us out to our car because it was always dark when we left. As we got up to the skywalk floor some friends came by hoping that their little girl could see Greg. She adores Greg and really wanted to see him. Many assumed that because Greg was in rehab, he was a lot better. I hated to disappoint her, but we had to say no visitors. It broke my heart to see her tears, but she could never have understood this very different Greg. He wasn't the man she loved and adored.

CHAPTER TWENTY-TWO

WHERE HAS GREG GONE?

"Therefore, gird your minds for action, keep sober in spirit..."
I Peter 1:13a NASB

February 7-8

I fell into bed that night with such a heavy heart. What was happening to my husband? Who could help me figure it out? There were so many pieces to this puzzle that made no sense. I did fall asleep by 11:00 as I was exhausted, and it had been a very long day. About 12:30 am the phone began to ring, and I woke up in fear. Since that first missed phone call in the middle of the night, I kept the phone by my bed each evening. The last middle of the night call had not been good news.

The person on the other end of the phone was no one I expected. It was my husband! I asked Greg why he wasn't asleep? Why was he calling?

He began a long chatter of all that was wrong, why he couldn't sleep, how the nurses wouldn't answer his page, on and on. I could not get him to stop talking or to listen. It was obvious that Greg was paranoid and very out of control. In my mind I could not comprehend that no one at the hospital had a clue what he was up to. I could not reason with Greg at all. After about twenty minutes I was able to finally, with much persuasion, get Greg to hang up the phone so I could call the nurse's desk and get him some help.

As I hung up the phone, I couldn't call the hospital. It felt like no one there had listened to me thus far, what good would it do now? My spirit was so fragile from the constant drain of this very different person. Instead, I woke up Kevin by phone and shared with him what Greg had said. As I was crying on the phone to Kevin, he took control and at my request called the hospital. He said he would get back to me. I laid back in bed, praying for Greg and for Kevin and that somehow God would intervene in this horrible time in our lives.

After a few minutes, my phone rang again. Kevin had reached the hospital, told them of Greg's bizarre behavior, (I think he yelled a bit at them too, for the neglectful care) and they unplugged Greg's phone. If they did anything else to help him that night, I don't know. No one from the hospital ever said a thing to me about it.

My sister and the Parr's would tell me later how difficult it had been that evening before as they watched Greg's behavior deteriorate. He was concerned about the woman in the hall (there was none), he made Dave P. watch a hockey game, not allowing him to look away for a minute. I think Dave will never forget that evening; he doesn't like to watch hockey. All of this behavior was not the man we knew. But the hospital didn't know who we knew and we were having a hard time getting any real help.

The next morning a "Care Conference" was scheduled for Greg. By now my emotions were totally spent. The conference is a meeting where the doctor, nurses, therapists, and any others connected with the case meet and discuss what's happening. The usual purpose is to make a decision about when the patient can go home; we were nowhere near that time. I wish that I could have been stronger, but I had spent so much energy on an individual basis to get some real help for Greg, to keep supporting him in his crisis state, and to help my kids process this strange time. I was totally exhausted and I could no longer hold back my tears.

I asked Scott Lucas if he would come down and sit in on the meeting. Pam also came, staying close to my side. Many times the patient is allowed to be there and is a part of the decision process. Greg was in no shape to participate. I did not go in and see Greg that morning, waiting instead until after our conference was over.

Amazingly, nurses were right there in the morning to speak with me. I was told I probably should not go in and see Greg but go directly to the conference. Which was already my plan. We stood outside the conference room, waiting for the existing meeting to end. Scott showed up and introduced himself as a psychologist from the clinic to the rehab doctor. I think the rest of the staff was surprised to see him there, but made no efforts to ban him. I could see that the rehab doctor was polite, but a bit surprised to see Scott. The doctor made no efforts to not allow Scott in the meeting. I probably would have hit him if he had.

We entered the room and I sat in a corner by Pam. They encouraged me to join the table, but I said I'd rather not. I knew I would not be able to speak. All of this difficult, heart-rendering, strange behavior had broken me. I don't know anyway else to describe it. The tears flowed and I could not stop them.

What was supposed to be a highlight in Greg's healing – doing therapy, getting stronger, becoming better had become – a horrendous nightmare. I resented the hospital and the lack of care and attention we were feeling. I had not expected to be blown off as I was, to have my husband mistreated, or to feel so helpless.

Pam relayed the difficult evening before, describing some of the disturbing behaviors we were seeing. The therapists all gave their reports. Physically he was doing well, but the tuna therapist was not pleased with his lack of direction and inability to follow orders. It galled me to listen to them. Could none of them see the mental struggle he was facing?

The psychotherapist from the unit said he was obsessing about religious things and was consumed with talking about the "end times." She spoke very disrespectfully about our family physician and her notes on Greg's chart. She said, "Who is this doctor? I've never heard of this person." We told her she was our family physician. It seemed that they were blaming everyone else, but taking little or no responsibility for Greg's crisis. He was, after all, in their professional care.

Gratefully, Scott dealt with their concerns. He assured them he knew this man well and that his baseline for life was a strong relationship with God. He spoke to them of the behaviors we were all concerned about and of our concerns about over-medication. The rehab doctor offered very little. In fact he could hardly look me in the face. 24 hours previous to this meeting I had confronted him about all of these issues. It was agreed among the professionals that a psychiatrist would need to see Greg. Dr. Bork was the psychiatrist on call and would stop by.

They told me it would be best not to see Greg. From a distance I peered into his room and saw him staring blankly out the window. It was a horribly painful time. I did not know how to bear any of this. We were in the hospital that was supposed to bring us hope and progress. We had just been handed a major setback.

I worried about Greg looking for me and my not being there for him. It was so incredibly hard to have come to this disappointing point after all the weight we had borne to just get here. We had survived incredible heart surgery, a major injury to his leg, two grand mal seizures, fevers, infections, near renal failure; the list could go on. Here we were at a point when it should have been easier, and it was the bleakest I had felt. I could not comprehend that things could be so awful. Right when we had finally got Greg's body back, were we destined to lose his mind? I prayed, "Please God, it can't be, it just can't be." My whole soul was pleading with God.

Dave Parr came by shortly after our meeting and I guess by the look on my face, he knew it was not going well. I told him about Greg's call, the meeting we had just come from and the news that none of us would be company for Greg that day. He wrapped his arms around me holding me close and said, "Oh Robynne, I am so sorry."

Pam filled him in on some more of the details. I didn't even know how to spend the day. Go home and be alone, waiting in fear? I knew I had to get a message to the kids to not come to the hospital. I believe Pam took care of that for me. The hospital also decided to post a "No Visitors" sign on his door. The other patient in Greg's room was moved. Greg was now alone.

I often wondered what was happening in Greg's heart and mind during this time. All of a sudden his family wasn't there; he was isolated in his room. Did he feel abandoned? I am so glad that he remembers very little of this time. We all learned a lot about the powerful overuse of medication.

Dave, Pam, and I sat in a little room and commiserated for a while, all of us extremely frustrated by the care, or lack of, that we had received. The one kind nurse that we grew to appreciate encouraged us to call and check on Greg as often as we wanted. I knew immediately that I could not call, but Pam, my always present, personal secretary, offered to make all the contacts. I gave the hospital permission and direction to answer all of her questions. I had had it with that place. I was totally out of fight for Greg; I did not know what more I could do.

After a while we decided to try to cheer up, not an easy thing to do. Greg's cousin had delivered pizza coupons to our family at the hospital so I offered to take Dave and Pam out to lunch. They had done so much for me and I didn't want to be

163

alone. Dave and Pam were great that day, letting me lead where the conversation was headed. They helped me process the strange events we were facing and assured me of their continued presence and support. They really were in there for the long haul. And it was a long haul.

I ran into a distant friend while out to lunch, and she asked how Greg was. She had heard he was doing better which physically he was. It was hard to explain what was happening, so I said he was coming along, but to keep praying for him.

After lunch I headed for the school to make contact with the staff and to find my kids. I barely entered the school and was flooded with tears and questions. I sat in Karen Snyder's office sobbing because the burden was so great. She listened with great compassion to this very difficult turn our journey had taken. She shared with me how different he was that day she sat with him while I went to lunch. It was good to know I wasn't the only one to see it.

I also was able to share with Dave Risdon. I needed some of the staff to understand the depth of this journey. Dave R. seemed to know the power and impact of medications and offered to hang in there with us and do whatever he could. Their support was tremendous. I know all of their hearts ached also. Many wanted to do something, but there was nothing they could do, or that I could do.

I headed home with the girls with such a heavy, heavy heart. I thought it would break, but I didn't really know what that meant. These days were for me the absolute worst. The initial surgery was so hard. The loss of the leg muscle had brought a real grief. The seizures had frightened us to death. Black Thursday had made us face his mortality. Now the mental battle loomed over all of these trials we had gotten through. I would tell Greg later that he really had a complete fix-over, head-to-toe.

CHAPTER TWENTY-THREE

NO DANCING WITH DADDY

"For we walk by faith, not by sight." II Corinthians 5:7 NASB

February 9

What made this part of our journey even more difficult to bear was the timing. This was the weekend of the annual Father/Daughter Valentine Ball. Early in Greg's illness we had hoped he would be able to go with his girls, even if in a wheelchair. The other dads had plans to wheel him in and around the dance floor. We were all hoping early on to celebrate by mid-February. When it became apparent that this would not happen, Brad, Kevin, and Scott A. took it upon themselves to escort their daughters as well as mine to the dance. Plan B had been for the girls to get all dressed up, stop by the hospital to show off their outfits to their dad, and then go to the dance. Now that was not even a possibility. Until further notice, we were not to see Greg. The hospital would let us know when Greg should have company. It was such a painful time for the kids, with no real explanation. How hard to have him away, and then to not see him. So far our time at the rehab hospital had not been encouraging.

When I was leaving the hospital that Friday and walking across the skywalk, Dr. Fetter saw me and called to me. He asked me with enthusiasm how it was going. I told him that it was not good. I explained to him that Greg was not himself, that he was obsessive and compulsive, and I didn't know what to do. In tears I explained some of the behavior we were witnessing and how I felt I could not get any real help. He asked me a few questions and then said he would check on him when he could.

I called Greg's mom Saturday morning and tearfully shared with her the difficult day before. She talked about the confusion Grandpa had from medication and seemed to understand. She was a wonderful support to me that morning.

In the meantime that blessing, called Teresa, decided to have a makeover party Saturday at her house for the girls who were going with their dads. Pam and Lauren, Teresa and Hannah, my girls, their friend Meagan and I gathered at her house. The girls had facials, oatmeal packs, hair highlighted, makeovers, manicures and their hair done. It was a most of the day affair and did a lot to lighten the load for Amanda and Abbey. They were able to dust off some of the sadness and enjoy the moment.

I vacillated between enjoying their joy and grieving for my husband. Even though there was laughter and lightness at the makeover party, I would still feel such a deep grief for Greg. My thoughts were never very far away from him, and I would feel the tears come often. No one in our lives had ever told us we had to be separated; it was so bizarre to know where he was, yet feel like he was a world away, which in a way he was.

When the girls were ready, Brad posed with them and the pictures were taken. They both were beautifully dressed, but the smiles came with difficulty. Still Amanda and Abbey were determined to make the most of the night. They knew that was where their dad would want them to be. Instead of one beautiful girl for a date, Brad had three: Hannah, Amanda and Abbey.

I spent the evening at home, catching up on regular household work. Luke was out with friends. I made some calls to family updating them on the current status of Greg. For the most part people did not know the psychological battle Greg was facing. Most were just as unsure what to say as I was, but they all kept praying. This was the first evening I had spent alone in a long time, especially alone at home. The regular comfort of peaceful time home alone did not come that night. I continually prayed for Greg, for Luke, and for the girls.

Brad had bought corsages for the girls at the dance, an extra kindness, and then brought them home about 10:30 pm. I was anxious to know how it went and to see if they were okay. I sat in my bed waiting for them. I didn't quite expect the response I got. They both burst into tears upon entering the bedroom. I thought they might be a little sad, having missed the moment with Dad, but I didn't expect the tears as they were coming.

Apparently someone who had been cruel to our family was at the dance and kept pursuing the girls for answers about their dad's condition. They did not want to answer any questions and they should not have had to. The fathers they were with did their best to protect them, but this man was determined. It broke Amanda's heart to have to try to speak with someone so cruel and unloving, someone who acted like he cared, but had clearly shown us that he didn't. One of the dad's who did not know this man said later that the man who had been bothering the girls looked evil. I did my best to comfort them and encouraged them to tell me about the positives. They did state that the MC mentioned Dad and asked for prayer for him.

Maybe there were some events that we just should have skipped; I still wonder about the Father/Daughter dance. Hopefully as time goes by, the good memories will outweigh the bad ones.

In the meantime, Pam kept us informed on the hospital status. The psychiatrist had diagnosed Greg with drug induced psychosis and sleep deprivation. From Friday on, a person was assigned to Greg's room to keep an eye on him and meet his needs.

The hospital told Pam that the psychiatrist had given Greg some medicine to sleep, and I learned later a tranquilizer to stabilize and slow down his mind. Sleep finally came for Greg and he dozed and dozed. Each time Pam would check, Greg was snoring peacefully – a real, deep sleep. Probably the first good sleep he had been able to get in two weeks.

CHAPTER TWENTY-FOUR

FINDING MIRAU

"But we had to be merry and rejoice, for this brother of yours...
was lost and has been found." Luke 15:32 NASB

February 10-12

Sunday morning we were informed that Greg was awake, eating breakfast, speaking more normally and that he would like to see his family. Luke, the girls, and I went in together that morning, our emotions excited and anxious. It was at once wonderful and difficult. Greg was much more like himself, so very happy to see us. He greeted us warmly, seeming so much more like the man we knew.

However, I was not prepared for how he looked. Somehow in that time frame he was supposed to be watched, Greg fell and received a bruised faced and a deep cut across his nose. What had happened? To this day I do not know the circumstances of his fall, although I asked many, many people. No one seemed to know what happened or no one would tell me.

I don't think Greg was aware of what had happened. He had obviously fallen since I had last seen him, but in the psychotic state he was in, he had no memory of it. Today he can vaguely remember a fall but cannot recall any of the details.

We were able to spend some good time with Greg that day, once again updating him on all that happened, trying to carefully choose our words. We all felt a cautious sense of renewed hope that we could now get back on track with therapy. We all were very ready for him to come home.

Monday morning I met Dr. Bork, the psychiatrist. He came into Greg's room and introduced himself. He asked Greg how he felt, did a few other inquiring questions and then looked at me. He said, "Is this more like your husband?" I said, "Yes." He said, "that's all I need to know." He told me that I knew Greg best and would be the best judge as to if Greg was getting back to normal or not. Finally, a doctor who again respected me, our family and our role in Greg's recovery. I had been so brushed aside the whole time we had been there. I was very grateful for that short, but important, conversation with Dr. Bork. It helped me greatly to once again feel my responsibility in my husband's recovery. I had been so unable to be heard or understood. Now once again someone was listening.

He told me how the medications Greg had been on put him on "overload". The tranquilizer he had given Greg hit the "reset" button of Greg's mind. It was good to see Greg become more and more himself again. Dr. Bork's diagnosis was exactly what I had been trying to convey to the doctor and specialists around Greg. From way back I knew Greg wasn't like himself, but no one really took me seriously. Now the specialist in the psychological field had stated that I would best know if Greg was Greg. Thank God!

Dr. Bork said he would check on Greg again, but for the most part his job with Greg was done. If we had any questions, or if any issues arrived, we were free to contact him. Of course all of this difficulty pushed back when we could leave the hospital. By now Greg himself was very anxious to get home.

Dr. Fetter took an active role in this part of Greg's recovery. When I had described Greg's symptoms to him in the skywalk that past Friday, he immediately contacted Dr. Eckman, the infectious disease doctor and the two of them looked closely for any clues. They were concerned that

Greg's brain could have developed an infection. Thank God, that was not the case. Dr. Fetter told me later he had gone to see Greg Friday night. He stated that he saw the posted "No Visitor" sign, but he said, "I rejected it and told the person with Greg, 'I'm his doctor!' "

I guess he visited at a good and a bad time. He was truly able to see how much Greg had deteriorated. When Dr. Fetter asked Greg if he knew who he was, Greg said, "Yes. You're the Antichrist." Greg also believed that his attendant was Osama bin Laden. If you remember, I did not speak with Greg that Friday. He had degenerated a lot since I had last seen him Thursday evening. Thank goodness that Dr. Fetter has a forgiving heart and a good sense of humor. He still likes to tease Greg about those comments. Greg just apologizes, stating that he was "out of his mind." I now tell Greg that any attempt to act goofy is no longer funny!

Monday was an even better day. It was now February 11th. We had been in the hospital for 1 month and a day. Greg was much more rested, clear-headed and able to focus. Therapy could begin again (everything had to be cancelled during the psychosis). That day Greg had occupational therapy, physical therapy, and a psychological evaluation. He was very determined about all of these appointments and worked hard.

One of the physical therapists was able to find a temporary brace for Greg to wear to assist with his walking. He needed something to keep the foot lifted with each step. It wasn't a perfect fit, but it was a welcome addition as it lifted that foot and helped with his walk. Everything was an adjustment, but Greg was determined to remind each part of his body what its responsibility was. Regaining strength from his head to his toe was top priority for Greg.

Special older friends stopped by that day. It was the first time they had come to see Greg and I was pleased that he was well enough to have visitors. Andy and Irmadel Williams were like second parents to Greg. It was comforting to have their presence in the room. It had been a while since someone new had come, and it reinforced for me that the support and the prayers were still out there for us.

Dr. Fetter came by also and took time to take Greg for a walk in the hall. He wanted to see for himself how Greg was progressing. I could tell that the medical staff on that floor could not quite comprehend what a heart surgeon was doing there, but John Fetter was our friend. He had invested a lot to see Greg survive, and he was there for us to complete the journey.

By Tuesday it was apparent that Greg was finally making forward, steady progress. Therapy sessions went much better, due in great part to Greg's head finally being clear. He could clearly hear and understand instructions and then complete the task. Dr. Bork felt that Greg could go home anytime as far as he was concerned. He told us he would make a note on Greg's chart stating so. Now we had to hope that all the therapists and the rehab doctor would be on the same page. A second Care Conference was scheduled for Wednesday morning.

Dave P. and Pam came early to be there for the conference. I knew Pam would not let me be in there alone. Scott L. was unable to get away from his practice that morning, but he had helped so much at the previous conference, and I knew if I needed any additional support he was just a phone call away. Thankfully, Greg was well enough to sit in on the meeting. As far as the therapists were concerned, he had passed all of their requirements. The psychotherapist admitted he was better, but was concerned with "gaps" she felt were in Greg. She recommended some continued therapy on a psychological level. I rejected her offer believing if the psychiatrist had no need to see Greg again, she didn't. We sat through that meeting, letting all of the specialists do their reports and then waited for the rehab doctor to confirm that Greg could be released from the hospital, which he did. He would need to write a discharge analysis, but that could be done later and mailed to us.

That afternoon they took Greg to Polinsky Rehab Center to have his leg "cast" to make a permanent brace for his foot. They would let us know when it was ready, and we would go back to get it. In the meantime, Greg was allowed to take the temporary brace home and wear it. It was not very comfortable for long term but assisted him greatly in being able to walk more normally. He would still need a walker for upper body support. He had lost a lot of strength, but we now felt with a bit of confidence we were going to make it.

So it was affirmed; we could take Greg home. Many offers were made by the staff concerning care questions we might have. They wanted me to feel free to call them with any issues we might have, but I knew I would never call them again. In my mind, they had failed us.

CHAPTER TWENTY-FIVE

HOMELAND SECURITY

"O Lord, I love the habitation of Thy house." Psalms 26:8a _{NASB}

February 13

On February 13th, 2002, 34 days after Greg first entered the hospital, we took him home. Even that "simple task" became an unbelievable ordeal.

Greg was so happy and excited. He missed home life and was very anxious to be back to a familiar place. As a family we finally felt like we had achieved victory. We knew we would need to come back for physical rehabilitation for his leg, but that could continue as an outpatient. The rehab doctor recommended a comprehensive list of follow-up visits that Greg should have, and the office was directed to make them. It also listed all of the medications he would need to continue on.

Greg was still on an anti-seizure medicine, coumadin, baby aspirin, and two anti-psychotic drugs. We were told by the morning nurse that his extra medication supply from the hospital would be sent home with Greg. We would not need to fill prescriptions right away. That was a relief and one less thing to think about. Because his leg incisions were not completely healed, they had me practice dressing Greg's leg, learning all of the right steps in assisting the surgery site healing. I didn't relish the idea of having to do this, but whatever it took, we would do.

Because "all of a sudden" we were going home, Dave and Pam headed out to our home to make preparations. Brad P. had already put in a new shower-head for us so that Greg could sit and shower. Mary Moline, a co-worker of Greg's, had given a shower chair to us. Dave installed a toilet seat lift that Pam just happened to have one from her collection of Grandma's things. Dave and Pam prepared everything. They picked up all my throw rugs so that nothing could be a hindrance to Greg as he entered our home. I was overwhelmed by the foresight they had and grateful that they took it upon themselves to make all those preparations. Dave went the extra mile to shovel out a path right by the house across the lawn so I could pull the van up close, thus easing Greg's entrance to the house.

Once again Greg had a roommate. Between his needs and ours, our leaving the hospital was pushed back later and later. Finally the paperwork was done and the release papers signed. An interesting note: On the day we left the rehab hospital, the admissions director came to speak with me. She was about a week and a half late with her admission information, but I graced her and let her do her thing. We went and sat in a waiting area, and I listened patiently as she walked me through the procedures and policies of the hospital. She asked me if I had any questions, but of course I didn't and any I had were too late to be answered. I told her we just wanted to go home. Her very late visit with us spoke volumes to me of the poor care we were receiving there.

The afternoon nurse came and I inquired about Greg's medications that we needed to take with us. She told me they had been thrown out and handed me a list of medicines I would need to pick up on the way home. I could not believe it. I told her the morning nurse had assured us that we would take home his medicines that were at the hospital. Because she could not retrieve them, I asked her to please call it in to our pharmacy and she did so. She did not offer this service, but she did comply.

We had repeatedly requested that Greg have physical therapy to practice getting in and out of a vehicle. Dr. Fetter had told us that of course they would do that, but it did not happen. Greg had done some stairs, going up and down, but not in and out of a vehicle.

We gathered our supplies for dressing Greg's leg. An earlier nurse had given us extra supplies to take with us. The afternoon nurse brought us some forms to sign and said, "You can take yourself out." I had never heard of such a thing. Wasn't the nurse supposed to wheel us to the door, assist the patient into the vehicle and wish us well? I was appalled, but by now the kids were at the hospital, and we wanted to go home. I did ask her which door we should exit at, and she answered me, and then went on her way paying no attention to us. So we helped Greg into his wheelchair and my girls pushed their dad to the door. There was no help and no assistance from anyone at the hospital. I was struck by this lack of concern and care. What if Greg were to slip or fall at their doorstep? I am sure this is probably not hospital protocol, and I know that many medical staff that heard of this later were also appalled. But for that moment we were on our own.

I asked Luke to go get the van and bring it to the front door. We had been in the hospital for five weeks, twisting and turning in all kinds of directions, with more specialists and caregivers than I care to remember. Yet here we were, on the final leg of our hospital journey exiting alone. It was very strange.

Because Greg had had no direction or practice in entering a vehicle with his bad leg, he had to figure it out. He basically crawled in on the van floor and then pulled himself up to the seat using his one good leg. The girls set the wheelchair back inside the hospital and we did not look back. It was an awkward moment, and it would have been nice to have help, but alas, we were alone.

177

Our first stop, of course, would be the pharmacy. It was wintertime, by now Greg was exhausted, and of course our prescription was not ready. I could not blame the pharmacy; they had just received a very long list of medications. I explained that we were heading home with the patient and they hustled to get things together. After about 40 minutes we were able to head home.

Once home we eased Greg into the house. He was still using the assistance of a walker which we had rented. Carefully and methodically we assisted Greg in and got him settled. Teresa and her son, Gus, were there to greet and welcome Greg home. It was a nice extra effort to not enter an empty house.

That one day had felt like a week long and all of a sudden a real fear welled up inside of me. For five weeks Greg had been under the care of a number of people. Now he became my sole responsibility. It was an overwhelming feeling. I still had a gnawing fear that something could go wrong; after all, so many things had, but I worked hard to focus on the good news that my husband and the kids' dad, was finally home.

It took all of our strength to assist his weakness in accomplishing the simplest tasks. I knew that I had a lot of responsibility in his care at that point, and I felt very insecure about it. It was a time of really depending on strength from God to even emotionally step up to the task before me. We had to stay focused and carefully think through everything we did. Amanda and Abbey became back-ups and double-checked medicines and procedures for me. That way we felt we would not make any mistakes. For a family who had never been on any medication, getting all those prescriptions correct really weighed on us. Probably for those who do it everyday it is no big deal, but if you don't know what you're doing and when you've had bad reactions to several medications, you don't want to make even the slightest mistake.

To be very honest, this was a scary time for me. But already God had provided an answer. My brother, Dwight, who lives in Alaska, had made plans earlier to come home. Being so far away and hearing the discouraging reports about Greg had made him afraid that I was to become a widow. He decided he needed to come home. He would arrive the next morning and be able to spend a week with us. My brother, Clyde, had already planned to meet him at the airport and deliver him to our house. One less thing for me to think about and a great kindness. Help from heaven when I needed it, and I really needed it.

That first night at home consisted of making Greg as comfortable as possible, getting him some good home cooking and giving proper medications. It probably doesn't sound like a lot, but for the girls and I, it was. We were concerned about Greg being comfortable, being warm enough, and having any need we could think of met.

Greg was so happy to be home; the sense and presence of a familiar place was as welcomed as a warm hug. The girls snuggled close to their dad, glad to be able to sit near him after such a long time. He placed his arms around them too and began the role of the father/caregiver that had been missing for 5 weeks. He maybe could not fulfill all the dad roles he was used to, but he could give hugs and kisses and that's what they needed most. Across the room Luke just grinned, he always knew his dad would make it back. Any other possibility was unthinkable as far as he was concerned. Coach Clark had told Luke to skip practice that day and just be home with his dad. I knew he was wondering when the team could see their coach again.

CHAPTER TWENTY-SIX

TRYING TO COPE

*"Come to Me all who are weary and heavy-laden
and I will give you rest." Matthew 11:30* NASB

February 14-16

I had fixed a mat for myself at the foot of our bed to be
near to Greg and meet his needs during the night. After much
effort he was ready for bed. Fortunately for us, we have a
bathroom right off the bedroom. That first night Greg tossed
and turned and had a lot of night sweats. I was up with him
eight times our first evening home.

His kidneys didn't hold out long yet, so there were many
trips to the bathroom. And then he would wake up and the
entire bed would be sopping wet as well as his clothes
because of the night sweats. I would strip the bed quickly and
find clean clothes for Greg. We would settle him back in bed
and in an hour or two, repeat the process.

I wasn't sure why the night sweats were occurring. No
one had said anything about them and I worried. Was there a
fever? What was happening with his body? We exhaustedly
survived that first night and I welcomed the morning light.

We worked Greg into the shower, grateful for the loan of
that shower chair, and he got cleaned up and dressed. Even
accomplishing these simple tasks was exhausting for him. He
wearily dragged his body to the living room and had some
breakfast. After taking his morning pills, we needed to
address the leg. I carefully unwrapped the leg (we wrapped it
in plastic during his shower) and removed all the bandages.
On the lower side of the outside skin graft was a slight
opening on the wound. The steristrip had to be soaked in

rubbing alcohol and then tucked into the wound. A topical antibiotic was applied over the graft and then layered with alcohol-soaked pads on the outside and dry pads on the inside graft of the leg. Then the entire leg was wrapped with an ace bandage to hold the pads in place.

Being careful to not allow any germs in there by wearing gloves, I painstakingly became the nurse for my husband. The girls were great to assist as needed, but none of us liked the job. By the time all of this was accomplished, Greg was exhausted and we got him back to bed for a morning rest.

Around 11:00 am my brothers Clyde and Dwight arrived. Hallelujah! Help had come! It was such an enormous lift to me to not be there alone with Greg. Even though he was doing well, I still felt an uncertainty that anything could go wrong and then what would I do?

When Greg woke up, he was pleased to see my brothers. He immensely enjoyed having them there. It became apparent from the start that Greg needed to talk about his journey and try to understand all he had been through. He would try to tell Dwight, but then be confused about what happened and the order of events that took place. We could tell fairly quickly that the information was overwhelming for Greg. We slowed him down and assured him that as time went on, it would all be clear to him. Letting him know that I had kept a daily journal helped him relax, knowing that when he was ready, he could read the entries.

Clyde stayed for a couple of hours, visiting with Greg and Dwight, and then we prepared to head to town. The hospital had sent with us a schedule of many follow-up appointments in the coming weeks and months. The first one was for a blood draw the first day he was home.

The appointment was scheduled at the clinic downtown, and we warmed up the van and headed for town. It was great to have Dwight to help Greg and me as the appointment became a bigger ordeal than we knew.

We had never really doctored at the Clinic and so were a little lost. Dwight dropped us off as close as he could and then parked the car. That walk in was a long one for a very weak Greg. We would stop often and let him regain some strength to go farther. After a long time, we made it to our floor. Greg took a seat and I checked us in, only to find out that they were not expecting us. I don't know where the mix-up came, but I explained that Greg had just come home, was extremely weak and tired and that he needed to have his blood drawn and tested. I showed the nurse my scheduled list of appointments and they told us to take a seat.

They accommodated us and the blood draw was made. The information was then sent to our clinic for our doctor to determine the amount of coumadin Greg would need. Greg was also scheduled for physical therapy that day, but after the walk to get his blood drawn, he had no strength to do any more. I called down to PT and cancelled the appointment. We headed home with Dwight assisting Greg on the journey back to the van. Getting Greg back out to the van and home again absolutely wiped him out. We all felt like we had had a very busy day. Once home I fixed us dinner and we settled in for the evening, catching up with Dwight and hearing about his family.

Again as evening approached, we gave Greg his evening medications, and all crawled into bed, extremely tired. The second night was equally restless for Greg. The night sweats continued and the need to get up for the bathroom awakened him many times.

One of the things we did was to put a night light on for Greg. Because he had not been in complete darkness for five weeks, he had a little anxiousness about it. We also wanted him to be able to see at night when he got up. Simple things like that helped the transition to home life a lot. It would have been nice to be more knowledgeable, but no one had prepared me in anyway for what the nights might be like.

I would be asleep and then hear in my drowsy state Greg calling my name over and over in an effort to awaken me. I would get up and assist him as needed. Many times I would pray over my husband, that God would comfort him, make him feel safe and allow him to rest.

Friday, February 15th, Greg had another appointment for a blood draw and test. Dwight and Amanda took Greg in that day. I stayed home and cleaned the house. It felt good to do some normal chore routines that day and feel like I was able to grasp a small portion of my regular life.

While in town, Dwight was able to pick up a handicap sticker for the van, pre-approved and suggested by the doctors. Dwight also purchased a cane for Greg and he found it really helpful. One of the therapists had told Greg which kind to get. It was easier to manipulate than the walker and gave him enough support. His strength was coming back as he ate good meals and relaxed in his own home. I believe there is so much stress just being in a hospital, and the body and mind spend so much energy trying to handle the stress. To be home allowed Greg to relax and allowed his body to spend the energy on the many aspects of healing it needed to do.

On Saturday we all breathed a sigh of relief; we did not have to go to an appointment. This was the first day in 37 that we didn't have to head to the hospital or clinic. We went through the morning routines of medications, shower, and dressing the leg. In the afternoon Luke had a basketball game. Because Dwight had never seen him play, I called and asked Dave P. if he would come and spend some time with Greg. He agreed to do so. I knew that Dave understood Greg's journey so well, had a great comprehension of all he had been through, and would be a great person to spend time with Greg. I think, too, it was good for Dave to spend some time with a much more focused, albeit tired Greg. He had seen the very different Greg probably more than he had wanted. I know it was a sacrifice for Dave to come that long way, but it was nice for me to have someone who knew the journey and in whom I could place complete trust.

Dave's coming allowed me to continue my support of Luke and the Marshall basketball team and allowed Dwight to see Luke play. It was nice to bring a report to the parents and kids that Greg was home and progressing in his healing. So many times, the games had been tearful and painful. This time we had some real hope. The girls came with us to the game. Amanda was a manager and Abbey a supporter.

CHAPTER TWENTY-SEVEN ·

THE FAMILY INFLUENCE

"I can do all things through Him who strengthens me."
Philippians 4:13 NASB

February 16-18

During Greg's illness, the basketball team had really struggled. They were 2-6 in an 8 game stretch. Quite often while we were in the hospital, before the team visited Greg all together, some of the members would come by, sometimes in groups, sometimes on their own, to see the family and me. I remember one day when Ian Kramer came by with a basket full of fruit. It struck me the courage of this young man to come alone, ask about Coach Mirau and bring us a gift. I knew he was worried about Greg.

Other team members would come by: Dan, Pete, Justin, Aaron, and Mark. These boys didn't know me all that well, but they cared and really wanted their encouraging Coach back on the bench. We were all praying for that day. Students from the school stopped in too and offered support to Amanda, Abbey, and Luke. It was really neat to see the passion and commitment the student body had and felt for our family. My kids commented on it a lot.

Marshall beat Hermantown that Saturday afternoon. The coaches allowed us to take the game tape home and Greg was immediately able to watch Luke and the others play. He had not seen a game in six weeks. It was a great moment for Luke and his dad to share in the comfort of our home. Looking at and analyzing the game, it felt like old times. Greg had missed so much, time he would never get back, and we

187

wanted to do all we could to help him catch up on the life that was happening outside of the hospital.

The week that Greg came home was also winter break, so the kids were able to be with their dad a lot. The winter Olympics were on TV and that became a great asset to pass the time. As Greg became stronger and stronger, it became more frustrating to be limited in what he could do. I was glad the kids could have some concentrated time with their dad. All of us would sit by him in amazement as we listened to his mechanical valve click with each beat of his heart. Even his heartbeat seemed much, much stronger, shaking his body at some points. Dr. Fetter assured me later that it was normal and not to be concerned.

Sunday morning, Dwight and the kids headed to church and I stayed home with Greg. We always had our morning routine of tasks to take care of. I could see the progress Greg was making on a daily basis. Food was bringing much needed nourishment to his body, and he could finally read and concentrate on the Bible and feed his starving soul. God was providing the healing on both levels.

Dwight provided extra parenting to our children. He played board games with them, interacted with, and teased them. Giving them the extra attention really helped the kids in their adjustment to having Dad home. Even though we were all delighted to have Dad home, it was not immediately the same; in fact it would never be fully the way it had been. I was grateful for the extra male influence and I believe it did a lot to comfort and bring security to all of us as we made adjustments and processed the past few weeks.

Monday morning, Greg had an early morning blood draw which was now being done in our clinic. This was so much easier because we could park close, take an elevator up and be right there. We had decided after his appointment to make our first trip with our new and improved Dad. We headed to my home place in Cromwell. This gave family a chance to see Dwight before he headed back to Alaska and was a safe, easy place to bring Greg and get him out a bit. A surprise awaited us all. Many members of the family were there to greet us. It was a beautiful, warm winter day made all the better by the loving welcome of family.

So many of them had not seen Greg since ICU days and were blessed abundantly to see this brother-in-law walk into the farm home on his own two legs with the aid of his cane. They had a wonderful potluck meal and everybody had a great visit. My brother Danny spent a lot of time right by Greg's side, supporting and understanding all that Greg had been through. In the afternoon, Greg laid down and rested. It took very little effort to take a nap, his body was just so tired.

Dave, Dwight, and I took a walk with some of the grandchildren of my parents to the far field of the farm. I wondered in my mind how many years it had been since the three of us had walked the farm. Many, many I'm sure. I really sensed the presence of my parents on that walk and their warm, smiling approval of how the family had rallied during this crisis. It felt so good for me, mentally and emotionally, to breathe the fresh air, to have a little space around me and to enjoy a scenery so different from the hospital.

There was security for me on the land, being back in the safety of my old farm life. Many times in my growing up years I would cross those fields praying and processing whatever was happening in my life. Here I was again, back enjoying the pure pleasure of the wonderful memories of growing up on that land. Walking with my brothers, I knew that my entire family carried with them the strong traditions of my parents. The love just flowed. Seven out of eight of my siblings had been to the hospital on many occasions and sat by my side in the lowest times. The eighth one had flown in from Alaska. They had reached out hand to hand with Greg, willing him to fight and get strong, bringing encouragement and love to their brother-in-law. They had also wrapped their arms around their sister, encouraging her to believe that we would win the horrible battle. Their influence on me was amazing.

When we arrived back at the house, the sun was high and warm and Greg was sitting on the deck surrounded by the remaining family. The sun brought much strength and healing to Greg's heart and soul that day. I felt the tears coming to realize that we could once again experience this kind of moment. Five weeks back I could never have imagined we would be able to share this kind of time again. Thankfully it was a warm winter and we basked in its mild temperature.

CHAPTER TWENTY-EIGHT

MOVING FORWARD

"For I have taken all this to my heart and explain it that righteous men, wise men, and their deeds are in the hand of God."
Ecclesiastes 9:1a NASB

February 19-26

Tuesday, February 19th, was a day without appointments. We were glad to just stay home, doing our routine and relaxing a little. That evening Marshall played Cromwell, my home team, in basketball. Once again the Marshall boys won. I believe the team was now able to relax a little and focus on their game because they knew Coach Mirau was home and healing. Their concentration did not have to be so divided. We debated about taking Greg to the game but felt he was just too weak and a bit vulnerable to do an outing like that. Our decision was to wait, Abbey volunteering to stay with her Dad. I called and checked on them both and they did just fine. Always in the back of my mind was what if something goes wrong, but I had decided the first day Greg went into the hospital that we had to keep living our lives, and as much as was possible, we were still trying to do that. Some of the people who knew Greg from Cromwell checked on his progress. It was good to know how widespread his support was.

Coach Clark had originally thought that they would have the team's parents' night at the Cromwell game but decided to postpone it a week. This gave Greg much needed time to heal. If at all possible he wanted to be there for Luke. Coach Clark wanted that too.

191

On Wednesday, Dwight needed to head back to Alaska and his family. We were so grateful for his visit, help, and support. We had been able to clean the garage a little and do some minor repairs around the house. His presence adding a lot of support in little ways that made that first week at home so much easier. Dwight and I went to town and did a few errands before he had to catch his flight. The girls stayed with their dad. I think Dwight was able to go home feeling a lot better about Greg and the progress he had made. I will always be grateful for that loving support he gave, the sacrifice his family made, and the bond we all built during that week.

We were told it would take a long time to regulate Greg's coumadin level and so constant blood draws needed to be taken. These were less effort with each journey down to our clinic. Greg became stronger and stronger and the confidence in his complete healing was increasing in my spirit.

On February 26th, Greg had two scheduled follow-up appointments, one with the heart surgeon, Dr. Fetter, one with the leg surgeon, Dr. Kaylor. Dr. Fetter's nurse had scheduled them back-to-back to assist with our trip down there. At 10:15 am we met with Dr. Fetter. As we walked back to his office, he proudly introduced Greg to his nurses, saying "This is the guy I was talking about!"

They all knew who Greg was and had heard of his incredible journey. They were very pleased to meet him. Dr. Fetter introduced him as the very popular Mr. Mirau. The first thing Dr. Fetter had Greg do was take a walk down the hallway with him.

Although the leg wasn't his area, he was keenly interested in how Greg was progressing. Inside his office he examined the surgical areas. The chest was healing pretty well except for a couple of little areas. There were some red spots that looked irritated, but he felt they would be fine given time. The groin area where they had inserted the surgical tube also looked good. Greg asked what the little holes were on his chest. Dr. Fetter explained how they had placed drainage tubes in his chest when the fluid had so quickly accumulated there. He also explained with a picture of the heart area what and exactly where the surgery on his chest had been done, where the tear had occurred on the aorta and what he had replaced in terms of the valve. The aortic tear was nearly four inches long!

Humorously enough, Greg had worn his Milliken sweatshirt that day. Dr. Fetter looked at it and asked, "Where did you get that?" Greg told him he had bought it off a clearance rack in a store in Iowa. We were soon to learn that Milliken is a college in Illinois where Dr. Fetter had first attended school. Quite a coincidence. Greg told him he always told his students that Milliken was a college where they taught students to milk cows! It was a nice, light moment. Overall, Dr. Fetter was extremely pleased with Greg's progress. He asked if he was eating well, encouraged us to continue as we were doing, and to never hesitate to call if we had questions. I did ask him how long the valve and synthetic aorta he had replaced would last. He said forever. These replaced parts didn't wear out. What a comfort to know that. I had thought in my mind that Greg would have to do all of this in another 5-10 years. That information was a like a breath of fresh air. We chatted briefly about other things and thanked him again for all he had done for us. I asked if he and his family would like to come for dinner sometime, and he said they would. With a promise to be in touch, we left his office to head for our appointment with Dr. Kaylor.

Dr. Kaylor is about as lighthearted and positive as they come. He was so pleased with the progress of Greg's leg. He looked interestedly at the brace that had been made for Greg and encouraged us to continue on. Therapy with Greg's leg would strengthen his efforts in balance and walking. But he told us, "The motor for the foot lift is gone. No amount of therapy can bring it back." That is what the brace was for.

We made an appointment to see Dr. Kaylor again in two weeks. Dr. Fetter did not need to see Greg again unless we had concerns. Greg was fixed and they were pleased. I did mention to both doctors that I was pretty unhappy with our care at the rehab hospital and the doctor there. Did I need to keep a follow-up appointment with that doctor? Neither felt there was any need to do so. I went home and cancelled the appointment with the rehab doctor. He had done very little to help us in our week and a half stay there. I didn't see any possible help he could give us in the future.

Another thing I did was to cancel rehab downtown and opt to go to the clinic in Hermantown instead. This was closer and much more convenient for us. It was also nice for Greg and I to not re-enter that hospital area that had been so disappointing to us.

CHAPTER TWENTY-NINE

BRINGING BACK COACH

"He who walks in integrity walks securely..." Proverbs 10:9a NASB

February 26

Our appointments were done early enough that we could bring Greg home to have a rest before the evening basketball game. Greg was determined to be at Parents' Night for Luke. This would be our first introduction of Greg back to the world that had long awaited to see him. Marshall would play basketball against Eveleth-Gilbert. I expected it would be an emotionally and physically exhausting event for Greg, but Luke and the rest of the team had waited a long time for this moment.

We brought Greg in by the back door close to Greg's office. As he sat at his desk I could already see emotions stirring inside of my husband. He had not been at his desk for a long time, and the last time was to call home and let us know he was headed for the hospital.

A few people who knew what was happening that night came back to his office to greet Greg. Kim and LuAnn Chart, my brother, Clyde, and family, and a few other close friends. We were so busy visiting with them that we were surprised when Luke came and got us. We were the last of the parents to be announced. Luke placed his arm around his dad and gave me an obligatory elbow as we entered the gym. I did not mind. This was Luke's moment with his dad. Coach Clark announced to the audience, "Luke Mirau with his parents and my favorite parents, Greg and Robynne Mirau." We entered the gym, Greg using his cane for support, to a standing ovation. The gymnasium erupted with cheers and applause.

195

Most of the audience was not aware that Greg would be there. I will never forget that magical moment for the whole school as this long-awaited, prayed for and cared for, teacher and coach, re-entered his school. It was an emotional night for all of us, the coaches, the family, and the team. I looked down the long line of players and parents and watched as Greg raised his cane in a salute of thank you for all the support. For Pete Newstrom, this was a highlight, telling me later it was one of the coolest moments for him.

Greg was engulfed in a barrage of hugs. Coach Clark came over to us and gave us each a hug and then asked Greg, "Are you going to sit on the bench, Coach?" I didn't realize until later that for most of the games while Greg was gone, no one sat in Greg's spot. They left his spot on the bench open waiting for his return.

Greg looked over at me with a sort of "Should I?" question on his face. I nodded yes. The whole team needed and wanted him there. Greg too needed to be with them. He was not at full strength by any stretch, but emotionally, mentally, and spiritually he needed to be with the team. I left Greg to find his spot on the bench and crossed the gym to sit with family and friends. We made it. The coach was back on the bench. My spirit was overwhelmed with the reality of it.

There was not a dry eye in the area of people I sat with. They told me later of the tremendous emotions they felt that moment Greg entered the gym. Everyone there was a part of the success story we were living. Everyone had contributed to this moment. They had prayed, sent money, visited, sent food, hugged the kids, brought comfort, and done whatever they could. Greg, sitting across the gym on that bench as the returning coach, was everybody's victory.

Looking across the gym at Greg I was touched to see a man visiting with him and shaking his hand. Dr. Mark Eckman had come to the gym that night too, enjoying the victory of this coach's life.

When we were interviewed later by the paper for the story they did, I told Rick Weegman that I always felt teary-eyed at the games during the national anthem; the coaches would be lined up and Greg's spot would be empty. That night as Greg took his spot on the bench and filled it with his healing body, the tears flowed again.

We settled into the game and watched as those boys played their hearts out for Coach Mirau. They won that game in a decided victory. The spirit of the team changed. These young men who had prayed so hard for our family, who had grieved at the loss of the coach on the bench, who had played so distractedly and struggled so much, had now regained their focus. They were there to play basketball and to play well. That night there were victories on many levels.

Coach Clark told me later reflecting on the team's year that even though the year started out great, the team struggled, back and forth, wins and losses. During Greg's low time they suffered a 4-game losing streak. He then added, "Bringing back Mirau added 10-15 points a game."

I was able to visit with several of the team members later that spring and they shed light on what they had really gone through. Pete N. told me, "The hardest part was just too hard. Coach Clark helped the team a lot to put Coach Mirau's journey into perspective: When to think about Coach and when to set it aside and play ball and have fun, because that is what Coach Mirau would want us to do. But when Coach Mirau came back to the bench at Parents' Night it was a lift for the team. Coach Mirau was the emotional and spiritual leader of our team, the 'heart and soul' of us. When Coach Mirau came back, something was right with the team again. I knew that night that we had not just won the game, but we had won the battle."

Dan Baumgartner, one of the captains of the team, shared about how the team was optimistic from the start. The season had started off really well, but they were dealing with Pete's recovery (he had been injured in football), then Coach Clark's son being ill, and then the crisis with Coach Mirau. He stated, "It was hard to focus and be excited about basketball when there were so many life problems occurring." He reminded me also about Pete's return to the team and then losing Geoff Ujdur to an injury. It was one more burden to bear as a team. "We were more than a basketball team," he said, "we were more of a basketball family. Coach Clark became our friend as well as our coach. While Coach Mirau was gone, a piece of the puzzle was missing. He is the 'father' of our team."

Ian Kramer, the center and a junior that year, reiterated what Dan had said. "Coach Mirau is the father of the team. Coach Mirau was not able to be there to back us up; we knew we had to back him up. We needed to play as a team. No one could do it alone." He went on to tell me that without Coach Mirau there they tried to create their own routine, but they could not. The routine was out of order without Coach Mirau. Ian shared the quote with me that Coach Mirau had given him, "It's not just playing the game, but winning when you need to" and said they placed it around the locker room. He then went on to tell me that when Coach Mirau came back he thought, "Here was a man who looks like he's been through the wringer, but he's been to the game and he's won," referring to Greg's medical battle. Ian also told me he wasn't much of a religious guy, but during those silent times before each game when he would usually psych himself up, he learned to pray.

I will say that these young men and the rest of the team impressed me so much with their maturity and confidence. Dan led the team that year in prayer for Coach Mirau before each game. The entire team became Luke's support system and he to them. During the darkest days they began to lose their confidence, but as Greg recovered it came back. Dan told me, "God gave us our confidence."

CHAPTER THIRTY

STRENGTHENING TIMES

*"Encourage the exhausted, and strengthen the feeble. Say to those
with palpitating heart, 'take courage, fear not.'"*
Isaiah 35:3-4a NASB

February 27- March 15

The next morning marked our first day at rehab at the
clinic in Hermantown. I went out to warm up the van only to
find we had a flat tire. Some days I wondered if the battle
would ever be easy. I quickly called our neighbors, Brad and
Teresa, and explained my dilemma. Brad was over in a matter
of minutes and drove us into rehab. He then picked us up
afterwards, brought us home, and then dealt with my flat tire. I
would hate to call him an angel (he does give me a lot of
teasing), but that day he was my hero – meeting a need that
we had. Great friends, great neighbors.

Greg liked his therapists at this clinic. He had two men
who really focused on him and helped us both understand
better the leg situation. They explained stretching exercises,
how to motivate the leg, and what the issues really were in
terms of recovery. They were great. Carol, the receptionist
down in the rehab unit, took a keen interest in our journey
and was always so helpful. This was a nice change for us
since our stay at the rehab hospital had been so
disappointing.

His next rehab time was scheduled for Friday. That
allowed us to be home on Thursday and those days just
home were very nice. Greg would nap twice a day, read, and
relax. I felt I could catch up on home stuff and the pressure

was off to always be going. It was wonderful to see on a daily basis Greg's body healing, readjusting, and gaining strength.

Abbey's pop concert was scheduled for that Friday night and Greg was able to attend. Everything we attended became a real celebration because we all knew that Greg could have easily have been gone from us. At the concert more and more people were able to greet Greg. They were so amazed at his comeback and amazed at how good he looked. He always said, "People say I look good, but nobody says I'm good looking." Most of us already know he's good-looking!

Rehab began in earnest, scheduling Greg for three times a week. The goal was to get strength in that leg, to work on issues of balance, and to find good positive ways to stretch those muscles that had been sitting dormant for so long. We already had hopes that Greg could be back at school after the Easter break. It was an aggressive goal, but one we all wanted to achieve. The school just said, "Come when you're ready."

The Marshall School was marvelous to us during our struggle. I never felt anything but loving support from the entire staff and student body. A few of Greg's closest co-workers kept in close contact with me. Mr. Schoer and Mr. Risdon came by on a regular basis.

I have asked Mr. Schoer and Mr. Risdon about our journey from their perspectives. Mr. Schoer had been refereeing the game with Greg that night the aorta tore. He told me he had no idea how bad the situation was and was shocked to hear what had really happened to Greg. He said he thought maybe Greg had the flu or something. With Greg gone, the office they shared was empty, and he was alone a lot. He told me, "I had concerns when he had the seizures and I was concerned about the leg, about how it would change Greg's life. But I always thought I would see him here again."

Mr. Risdon shared about how worried the school really was. On his first visit to see Greg at the hospital Greg was conscious and joking. But on the second visit, Greg only opened one eye and then closed it again. He said, "I felt some need to prepare myself for him (Greg) not to make it. I prayed for him."

Thankfully those prayers were answered. Mr. Risdon is Abbey's orchestra teacher, and he kept a close eye on her for me at school. I know he and Mr. Schoer as well as the administration all offered their time and support to our children at any time. Mr. Risdon saw Abbey distance herself a little, but was able to allow her space and yet keep her focused and encouraged. He also told me, "These situations make you think about life, about what is important and what is not important."

In May, Mr. Schoer, Mr. Risdon and Mr. Mirau spent an afternoon fishing on the St. Louis Bay. It was their own little victory celebration.

Karen Snyder, the Marshall Middle School administrator, came to the hospital quite often. The first Saturday she came bearing food. (John Parr was pleased!) Reflecting back with me one day, it was obvious how much Karen had carried our burden. She had been there the first night with Chris Johnson. She had worked with Greg to solve immediate school needs. She said she was amazed how composed and confident Greg seemed. When I wasn't falling apart she wondered if either of us knew what we were facing. She did remember that the girls were crying. One of the school's first responsibilities after finding a sub was to craft a statement to give to the student body. They wanted to be honest, but not scare the school. The staff did a nice job of honestly updating the school body without over-alarming anyone. They also

203

helped keep visitors at bay. Karen also saw Greg in some of his difficult days. She told me watching Greg face all the setbacks made her feel unsure of his recovery. Many days she looked outside of her office at that empty post and continued to wish him back. She told me that she held on to what I had said – that God had a reason for all of this. God had a plan.

The student body signed poster board size get-well wishes for Mr. Mirau. He had a great time reading the notes from so many students. He also received an autographed hockey stick from the Marshall hockey team and autographed basketballs from both the JV and Varsity boys' teams.

In the meantime, the Marshall boys' basketball team was in the playoffs and still winning. During Greg's hospital stay the boys team had lost to Proctor and Chisholm. These were now two teams they had to face and beat in the playoffs to be able to continue their journey to state.

After our initial entrance into the gym on Parent's Night, Greg made each and every game. He would sit on the bench at all of the games but was careful to keep himself composed. He called it a quiet kind of excitement; he just didn't want to not take care of himself. It was difficult to know how much freedom to take emotionally. Everything was still pretty overwhelming and we both wanted to be careful.

I watched in amazement, surrounded by a host of friends at the gym of St. Scholastica. The excitement of the team was so cool. These boys were focused and ready. That night they played very well and beat Chisholm in their continued streak of winning. Luke too had a good game and played well. They were so bonded as a team; it was amazing to watch. I heard the coach of Chisholm had said that the one team he didn't want to face in the playoffs was Marshall because he knew they had something to prove, and they did.

After the win, amongst the jumping and joyfulness of the team members, were Luke and his dad embracing each other in a wonderful celebration of victory, both on and off the court. The girlfriends sitting all around me had tears in their eyes at that picture of father and son. Now the team had two games ahead of them to clinch the section championship. But for us, it was still one day at a time.

We kept our second appointment with Dr. Kaylor, and again he was very pleased with Greg's leg. He examined the new permanent brace and pronounced it perfect. His work with us was done. Because the leg had healed so well we were able to back off on the daily wrappings. He encouraged him to wear a support stocking of some sort and to continue with therapy. Strike two doctors off of our follow-up list.

The second section playoff game was that night. This one would be played at Romano gym on the UMD campus. Each game attended was an exertion of effort for Greg. We always tried to drop him off as close as possible to limit how much walking he needed to do, if at all possible avoiding many stairs because his balance still wasn't what it needed to be. It always seemed like such a long walk into the gyms, but the walking was coming a little better, and he used the cane less and less.

Tonight's game was against Proctor, Coach Clark's former high school. There was a lot of anticipation. Grandma and the Mirau family were there along with some of my family. All of us were supporting Luke and the whole team and just itching to keep the celebrations going. Everything finally seemed to be going right for them, and they were reveling in it. You could see and feel the excitement on each teammate's face. If they could beat Proctor, there would be just one more game to win before reaching the state tournament. It would be the first time in Marshall school history for the boys basketball team to go to state.

They beat Proctor that night. Luke scored ten points in the come-from-behind win. This was the second time they needed to rally for the victory. Their confidence was clearly growing and their hopes were soaring. This group of young men had grown up so fast through the journey of their coach and the difficult year. I inwardly kept praying that going to state would be their reward.

The next day we went to see Dr. Prusak. She was the one who would determine the withdrawal of Greg's anti-seizure medicine and the anti-psychotics. We told her we were anxious to be rid of them. While Greg was on them he could not drive a vehicle and he was ready to become a bit more independent.

She heard us well and wrote out withdrawal times and schedules. In fact she took one medication away that day. Then she wrote us a schedule for getting off the others. Beginning with going down to once a day, and then not at all; one medication at a time. If all went well, meaning no ill effects, Greg would be able to drive again. Dr. Fetter had commented early on that because Greg's left leg suffered the injury it would not affect driving as long as he had an automatic. I'm proud to say that today Greg can drive a stick-shift – one more victory!

Greg had been home for a month now. I was still sleeping on the floor, not wanting to disturb the leg and also trying to get his nights and days back where they belonged. The nights were getting better. Greg would sleep a better stretch and then get up two or three times a night rather than seven or eight. We were making progress on the sleeping front. We began the withdrawal of the medications. There were three to come off of. By mid-week he was off the second, and by the end of the week the third. Greg showed no signs of seizures and no psychotic behavior. His mind, emotions, and body were coming back in line, the way they should be.

CHAPTER THIRTY-ONE

REAL VICTORY

"I know that there is nothing better for them than to rejoice and to do good in one's lifetime." Ecclesiastes 3:12 NASB

March 16-19

The last game of the playoffs was against Pequot Lakes, a team they had never played before or seen. My ever-consistent support group sat there in great anticipation. People from both of our families had now begun to regularly make the trek to the games in support of both Luke and Greg. We sat there huddled together, hoping for the best for this team. These boys already knew they had witnessed a miracle in the amazing healing of their coach, but now they were hoping for another. Anticipation was rising, but so was their confidence. With each victory they gained more. It was now part of Greg's routine at the end of each game to be in the locker room with the team mostly handing out hugs. The team would line up for the affirming touch of their coach. They beat Pequot Lakes 58-41 and secured their trip to state.

What a celebration! The culmination of a very tough season – ups and downs, fears and hopes, good news and bad news, victories and defeats – had given way to the final success story. The team and the fans were elated. I watched the coaches and team hug each other in amazing celebration. The gymnasium floor was flooded with well-wishers, all embracing one another in this terrific moment. The emotions were so huge. I felt so blessed that God had seen fit to let Greg be here for this moment. I knew that this was one of those memories that will stay strong in many minds for many years to come.

In the locker room afterward, Coach Clark congratulated the team on a great victory and a great season. He handed out the medals to each of the participating players. The managers also received a medal. He then had two left for the coaching staff. There were four coaches, the JV and 9th grade coach stepping up and assisting Clark in Greg's absence. But Coach Clark already knew where the last medal would go. He handed it to Greg with the smiles and approval of the whole team and coaching staff. Greg had missed almost half the season on the bench but not in their hearts. In the hearts of the team and coaches, and yes, even in the school, he was present at every game. He, in his own quiet way, had won his own medal and shared totally in the victory of that night.

When many of the team members were in the 8th grade and under Coach Mirau, he had travel pillows made for the team by LuAnn Chart. At the end of that season while he handed them out, he told the boys they could use them on their trip to state. Mark Stauduhar came up to Coach Mirau that night stating, "I am going to find that pillow!"

We had been asked to give interviews that night to the Duluth News Tribune whose sports reporter, Rick Weegman, wanted to write Luke's and Greg's story. I waited with family and friends in the gym after the game for the guys to be done with the interview. Luke came and found me saying that Rick wanted to talk with me too. I did some clarification in the order of events and answered the questions he asked. After the interview we brought Greg home, knowing that a great story was coming. No, maybe more correctly, that a great story had just happened.

Before the game, the photographer had asked about getting a picture. Luke was concerned that they hadn't taken the picture he thought they were supposed to. He had no need for concern; the photographer captured the perfect picture of Greg and Luke embracing after the game. So many people commented to me about that picture, father and son in the embrace of the biggest victory of their lives. Luke really never doubted that his dad would be there, and in that moment his faith had been rewarded. Friends had a print made of that photo and framed it as a gift for Luke's graduation. It hangs proudly in Luke's dorm room at college.

The article was published the following Tuesday, March 19th – our 19th wedding anniversary. Rick did a wonderful job of capturing the team's journey, the Mirau journey, and the victory we had all experienced.

I brought Greg to school that afternoon for the send-off assembly for the boys basketball team. He sat in the front row of the auditorium with the other coaches and team. Coach Clark welcomed him back to the school and he was given another standing ovation. Many of the students and staff had not seen him yet. Really only the basketball families and administration had made the connections back with Greg. After Coach Clark spoke a few words he called Dan Baumgartner up front. Dan announced and congratulated Mr. and Mrs. Mirau on their anniversary and we received more applause.

Marshall has a "Topper Tunnel" where all the kids form a tunnel for the team heading to state to run through. I walked to the far end of the building while the tunnel was forming. I wanted to watch the boys come out through the tunnel and get some pictures of this great moment. They came running through happy, excited and pumped up for the game. The team headed outside and loaded the bus for their first trip to state.

A few minutes after they were loaded, a parent came and summoned Greg and I to the bus, stating casually that someone needed something. As we approached the bus, the entire team came off the bus singing "Happy Anniversary" to us and presented me with a corsage. What a terrific group of young men, a great team of talented athletes, and thoughtful besides. We assured them we would see them in Brainerd.

You can spend anniversaries doing a lot of things: trips, dinners, quiet moments spent together. But in all of our years together, that day was the best celebration we ever shared.

Scott Anderson had volunteered to drive us over in our van and Kevin would drive us back. He and Pam came later with the rest of the families. That made it nicer for me. This would be the farthest away from the doctors and hospitals we had gone since January 10th. It was nice to have the support of another adult. We situated Greg in the back with his leg elevated. I was still insecure about a lot of things concerning Greg and was grateful for the guys' extra effort with us.

The team's dream ended that night with a defeat to the opposing team. They lost in their first round at state. It was a disappointment, but I could see in their faces that they were not defeated. The whole season had taught them so much and they had endured a very difficult year. I believe for the team the victories were about so much more than the game. These boys, along with their coaches, had won a victory of life. The coach that always loved them, hugged them, teased them, and encouraged them, was back. For the 2001-2002 season, their real victory was here to stay.

Dan B. stated, "I feel so in debt to the experience I've had at Marshall. It's tough to watch people you love hurt. It's hard to lose games. But the impact of this year made me a lot more responsible. Mr. Mirau's journey put things in perspective. It was a growing up experience."

Ian told me, "Through much hardship there is much strength." After the loss he was crying on Coach Mirau's shoulder feeling so bad. He said about the loss, "It seemed useless, but hugging Coach helped me regain the focus; it was all right."

210

It was interesting for me post-basketball to talk with Luke about his feelings of this journey. He told me the mood at basketball was always a little solemn. He would get asked all the time if he was going to the hospital. He said when he did see his dad, Greg would grab Luke's thumb letting Luke know that he knew he was there. He told me, "Dad squeezed so hard, it was so strong, I knew he would not die."

Luke also talked about parent's night. "I wasn't just bringing out my dad. I was bringing out my hero," he said. "The gym is different without Dad, without the sound of his voice. Dad had a lot of obstacles to face, but he took the challenge and faced them head on. He is back living life."

One of the hardest things for Luke has been the loss of Greg's leg muscle. The "jump" isn't there and not everything can be done the same, but he still comments on the progress his dad is making.

Pete N. said it was a "year of sacrifice for the team, big and small. Like praying no matter what you believe. Mr. Mirau's recovery was surprising but not surprising. I knew he would not tell the team to 'not give up' and then give up himself."

Adam Machones probably had the strongest feelings about the season stating, "I seriously believe that one reason we didn't achieve our goal of a state tournament in the following season was because the Big Guy was not coaching. He was not on our bench or in our everyday practices. Just the other day we were having a bad practice, Coach Mirau came into the gym for five minutes between reffing games. He helped Coach Clark for five minutes, standing in the door of the gym. The impact he made was phenomenal. We ended up having our best practice of the year by far. Everyone noticed the impact that he made. Mr. Mirau has the ability to make everyone around him better. He does this everyday."

CHAPTER THIRTY-TWO

MORE HEALING

"So teach us to number our days, that we may present to Thee a heart of wisdom." Psalms 90:12 NASB

March 20 and on...

On March 20th, I was finally able to crawl back in bed beside my husband. His leg was fully healed and he was sleeping pretty well at night. One thing that first impacted me was how much his body would jerk at night. It was unsettling for me and I felt uncertain as to why it was happening. A conversation with my friend, Gail, brought light to the subject. As I was updating her on Greg's recovery and my relief at having dropped medications, she realized that was the answer. His body was still withdrawing from being on all those medications, thus the jerking motions. They did not last too long and the worry was temporary. I was grateful for her insights.

During that last week of March, the medical bills began to come. We actually had very good insurance, but considering all Greg had gone through we knew we would have a fair sized bill. On that Monday, Greg asked me what I thought we should do for a first payment. I looked at him and said, "God is going to pay those bills." And God did. That day in the mail we received a card and a check from some good friends for $500. Greg had taught their kids in school and been a positive influence in their lives; they just wanted to say thanks. The next day another card arrived, this one from our kids 3rd grade teacher, again with a note of encouragement and $50. We also received a check for $100 from a family we had known when he taught at Beaver River School. It was amazing.

I brought Greg to school on that Thursday so he could check his e-mail and begin preparations for going back to teaching. While he was there, the Marshall Head of School, Marlene David, saw him and asked if he was going to be there for a while. He said yes and she said she would be back in a bit. She did come back and gave Greg an envelope. Inside was a check for $7,500! It was given to the school by someone so they could give it to us anonymously. Amazing. We paid off the bills with extra to spare! We were so overwhelmed. Marlene said something to Greg about not knowing what your impact is on people and how they want to help back. We wrote a note back to that anonymous giver and the school delivered it for us.

One and a half weeks later Greg drove us to his mom's house for Easter Sunday. We had not been to his family's since we had come home from the hospital. We kept in close contact with them, but just hadn't gone home. This was Greg's mom's time to welcome her son. She was so grateful for his life, and so was the entire family. It was a great celebration to be with them and I felt proud that God had given this son back to his family, especially to his mom. She had prayed so hard and often for us all. She told me much later that when she was praying one day, God came to her and showed her that Greg would make it and be okay. It was a moment of special peace for her and helped her to survive all the difficult days of our journey.

Every member of Greg's family had been there for us. Flo and Rod from the first night on. Greg's mom, Joe and Bev, Kirby, Patti and family had all stood by Greg's bedside, sat with me in surgery waiting, and offered many kindnesses. Many times their encouraging statements were the words I held on to.

On Thursday, April 11th, three months and one day after Greg's aorta tore, he went back to school to teach. He stood at his post by the gymnasium welcoming kids back to school. The miracle man was back at it.

There were, of course, apprehensions about teaching. Greg is a health and phy-ed teacher, a very physical, moving job. There was uncertainty about how it would work in gym class because Greg usually plays the games with the kids. Could his changed leg handle all that was required? He knew the only way to find the answer was to try.

His schedule of teaching allowed him to come home by 2:00pm each day. This was helpful because the body was still doing a lot of healing, and he became very tired. Each day he would come home and get a midday nap. This gave him strength for the next day of work. For the first several weeks Greg taught two days, took off Wednesdays, and then would teach two more. Because teaching is such an emotionally draining job and Greg puts so much into so many people, this really helped his re-entrance into the working world.

Mr. Schoer and Mr. Risdon kept close tabs on Greg for me while he was at school, always attentive to how he felt. It reassured me to know they kept a close eye on him because for the first time in three months, I couldn't.

I took a day away one afternoon and Greg came home to an empty house, the first time since he came home from the hospital. I was learning that everything was an adjustment. Although he did fine, he began to feel some anxiety about being alone, way out in the country. The anxiety seemed to increase over the next few weeks. It was not overwhelming in anyway, just kind of a constant nag inside of Greg if he was alone for a length of time.

For his home rehab, Greg did a lot of walking – usually on the road. We began taking walks together in the woods. We have some wonderful trails on the property that go up and

215

down the hills along the lakeshore. These treks in the woods ended up serving two purposes. The actual physical walking, stepping over tree trunks and going up and down the hills was very good for Greg's rehab. It forced him to use balance, stretch muscles, and accommodate a variety of stepping forms. We both really saw him improve in the use of his leg through these walks. We continued these walks for about two months.

The other thing that happened was the processing time. Away from people, our children, and alone in the woods, Greg began to ask me a lot of questions about what had really happened. What was that incredible journey he had been on? It was in these conversations that a real grief inside of Greg was able to come out. In those woods, away from the world and the busyness of life, Greg was able to release fears, sadness, uncertainty and apprehensions that had bottled up inside of him. The grief came and was allowed. His life had been changed; he had suffered a loss of muscle. Each day he was forced to make physical adjustments and he had done so. Now was the time for the emotions to catch up.

Though I am not accustomed to handling tears from Greg, it did my heart and his heart good to have those sad times together. We would pray and ask God to complete the healing from the inside out. The more we walked and processed, the more the healing grew. Within a month, the anxiety left. It has never returned.

No one ever told me I would need to help Greg work through these things, maybe no one knew. I would often bounce my conversations with Greg off of Kevin. He would always affirm what we were doing. He has a great way of helping both Greg and I feel comfortable with the healing journey. So much of what was happening was what needed to happen. It was comforting to have the support of a good friend helping us along the way.

Our kids became accustomed to our daily treks, and the girls would finish preparing supper while we walked. Greg could process whatever was on his mind, and then we would come home and have a great evening together. I think it is important for people to see the whole picture of healing. It is so much more than physical. At one of our appointments Dr. Kaylor told Greg that healing is 80 percent in the head. He is right. Greg's great attitude and strong faith, plus the love and support of so many people, all brought forth a tremendous healing one day at a time.

A good friend, Craig Sterle, (his son John was also on the team) told me early on after Greg came home from the hospital to give ourselves a full year to heal, not to make any assumptions or to entertain any fears until we reached that year goal. Sometimes I would find myself worrying or anticipating too much of what might go wrong. I would get caught up in worrying about tomorrow or some issue of the day. Pushing forward a deadline to evaluate Greg's progress was good advice. It helped me to slow down my expectations of healing and processing, to allow us to take the time. My brother, Clyde, says of many things in life, "It takes the time it takes." This was true for Greg's complete healing. However, I longed for January 10, 2003 with all of my soul. I wanted to reach a year and have this frightening ordeal that far behind.

CHAPTER THIRTY-THREE

A NEW SEASON

*" 'Because he loves me', says the Lord, 'I will rescue him; I will
protect him, for he acknowledges my name. He will call upon me,
and I will answer him, I will be with him in trouble. I will deliver him
and honor him. With long life will I satisfy him and show him my
salvation.' " Psalms 91:14-16 NASB*

The verse I quote at the beginning of this chapter was
scripture God gave to both Pam and Pastor Ryan. It became
their promise from God for Greg. It is now framed and sits on
Greg's desk as a reminder of God's faithfulness.

Pastor Ryan and his wife, Krista, sat down with me and
reflected on our medical miracle. Ryan recalls really wrestling
with God, pleading with God to not ask him to do Greg's
funeral. He said to God, "I am not available for a funeral for
Greg!" It is wonderful that God heard that! They both shared
how it challenged their faith. Ryan remembers knowing that
"though God slay Greg, yet he would trust Him" and knew that
God would also equip Ryan to take care of our family. Many,
many times Ryan prayed over Greg at the hospital and
always assured him his family was taken care of, and we
were. Krista admired Greg's trust also saying she has never
seen Greg bitter or prideful. I didn't know it then, but as a
young man Ryan watched his own father battle through
serious injury. Pastor Ryan was definitely God's man for our
family in this battle.

When I interviewed Dr. Kaylor, I shared with him Pastor
Ryan's prayer over Greg and the bed lifting Greg's body
toward him. Dr. Kaylor had been the one to move Greg into
that type of bed. I told him Ryan was pretty alarmed, thinking

that he was raising Greg from the bed. Dr. Kaylor told me "your pastor's praying did raise Greg up." He went on to say that statistically, Greg should have died. When the leg complications occurred, the dead muscle caused the muscle cells to rupture releasing myoglobin, which is toxic to the kidneys. The body tries to handle this, but very quickly there can be a multi-system shutdown. Dr. Kaylor also knows that Greg is a miracle. He told us once, "I meet the nicest people for the wrongest reasons." We are glad to know Dr. Ken Kaylor, even if we didn't always appreciate the reason why.

As summertime approached, and we embraced a new season, we watched Luke graduate from high school. He and his dad shared the stage together for Baccalaureate. Luke did a reading and Greg offered an invocation. Each experience became a victory for our family. I remember feeling much more emotional about Greg and Luke sharing the moment together than I did about Luke finishing high school.

Many friends came alongside us and helped us with our open house for Luke. It was so wonderful. Many people have commented to both Greg and I on the amazing friends we have and are really impressed by them. It's true. We are blessed in abundance in loving, giving friendships. Every need was met by friends or family in our journey.

Greg's body continued to increase in strength. He found he was able to do more and more. In early June, we scheduled a day for Dr. Fetter and his family to come for dinner. On a warm Sunday evening they pulled into our yard and entered our home.

Greg had been to see Dr. Pusak in the past week because of a hard lump we found at the end of his surgical opening. She thought it might be the zyphoid and explained how it may have been cut. Unsure, our doctor ordered an x-ray. It worked out that Greg had the x-ray at home to bring back to the doctor. Because Dr. Fetter was in our home, he knew immediately what the lump was. They had cut through the zyphoid and in the re-healing that was where it ended. Nothing to fear! Yeah! Both doctors had nailed it.

The whole journey was a victory for both of our families. Greg had gone on-line and found a Milliken sweatshirt for Dr. Fetter. It was fun to give him a gift. We were, and remain, so grateful for all he did for us. The way he stuck with us above and beyond his hospital responsibilities. (Even doing medical checks in our home!) He took the risk to be personally involved in every aspect of our journey and prayed for healing for Greg and our family. He is a hero to me and to all of us. It was a nice evening, good to meet his family and to thank them for the time they give daily to allow their dad and husband to be there for so many others.

Dr. Fetter did tell us that the privacy act was a problem for him while Greg was in the hospital because he was daily bombarded with so many people asking him about Greg. He told me that when he first saw Greg he remembered thinking he was a young man for this condition. But after the CAT scans he realized, "Greg had lived his whole adult life with a fatal condition."

Life began to take on a more normal feel by mid-summer. Greg was working with his guys on his summer job. He was still making adjustments to being comfortable with his brace, but overall, everything seemed to be improving. The doctors had told him to stay off ladders and planks for the first summer, which he did, painting only from the ground.

The fall brought Luke leaving for college and a new school year for Greg, Amanda, and Abbey. We continued to see steadfast progress in Greg's healing journey. He would gain more energy, seem more like himself, feel more confident with his body and all of the changes it had been through.

Greg decided in early November to not join the coaching staff of the basketball season that year. He still tired easily, and we felt that to be at practice six days a week on top of school responsibilities was just too much. Although the guys were disappointed, we made every game with Greg on the sidelines yelling their names, encouraging their plays and going to the locker room after each game giving them hugs and high fives. I consider him the "Honorary Coach". I know they do too. The other coaches also look for his encouragement and support. Coach Clark has commented to me more than once that those after-game visits are just what the team needs.

CHAPTER THIRTY-FOUR

EACH DAY'S A GIFT

"...you have tasted the kindness of the Lord." I Peter 2:3 NASB

In mid-December, 11 months after Greg's aorta tore, he was back on the Marshall basketball court, refereeing a basketball game. I wasn't sure I was fully comfortable with this, but the doctors all told him he could do whatever he felt like doing. I did not go and watch him; for me it was a psychological fear. But you know what? He did it, and he did just fine. In 11 months, my husband had regained everything that illness was threatening to take. He is a walking miracle, and many know it.

On January 10th, 2003, we marked our one-year celebration of Greg's life. We had made it through that terrible, horrible year of fear and uncertainty. For the first three months of the year following that day, the girls and I would mark what was happening a year ago. It was remarkable to all of us what had transpired and how much healing had taken place.

On February 8th, 2003, Amanda, Abbey, and their dad attended the Father/Daughter Valentine Ball and they both danced in their father's arms. He was back and they were enjoying each moment. The leg and foot were still adjusting and Greg worked hard to improve their strength. Dr. Kaylor said Greg is off the charts in recovery, and doing far more than they ever expected. We thank God for this.

I stayed home alone that night. Luke was down at college and my heart just rejoiced that Greg and his girls were sharing this moment. I wondered how the dance moves were going; Greg's foot had been pretty sore lately. But I need not worry; Amanda told me her Dad was teaching dance moves to others. Alongside them were Brad and Hannah, Kevin and Kassie and Kenzie, Scott and Lauren, Dave and Megan, all celebrating the wonderful evening together. He had missed one dance, but he was back for the next. I know my girls will never forget that horrible time without him, but the fears of that year will fade as they are replaced with the joy of the last dance.

On a regular basis Greg, the girls, and I run into people who ask us how he is doing. Each time we answer with a little more confidence: He is doing great, healing well and making progress. So many people have their own stories to share: how his illness impacted them, how they prayed, what they feared. It is amazing how our journey has crossed the path and affected the lives of so many others. I tell people all the time, I don't understand the purpose of Greg's trauma, but I do hear and am learning a lot about the impact.

Most of us don't ever realize if or how our lives are affecting others. In the mid-stream of our lives, God showed us, and we are still learning that we do affects others. There is a purpose and a plan and a promise.

Geoff Ujdur was reminiscing about that frightful year remembering how Greg had teased the boys when the team visited. "At first I didn't remember his propensity to be a practical joker and it scared me half to death. I (feel) this is evidence of the reason that I personally was able to get through this trying time of my life. Seeing Greg be so positive and courageous in the face of death made me realize that not having a life threatening injury was something of comparable ease. I was missing a season of basketball, not my way of life. As the team rebounded from early struggles around this time of the season, I believe that it was Greg's positive attitude that enabled the team to ultimately achieve this success at the end of the season on the run to state. All this adversity made our team come together and I think it made us stronger, and we felt that no team had been through this and in turn we had an advantage."

Greg is a success story, not just for his family, team and school, but for the doctors who worked so hard to save his life, who intervened to deter the complications that kept cropping up in their faces, who were thrown together to solve complications that usually don't occur together, and who needed to face their sons and daughters each night and assure them that Mr. Mirau will be back. And he is.

As frustrated as I was at points, it seems that life balances out. On more than one occasion, I was asked or encouraged to file a lawsuit against some of the errors made in Greg's care. That would never be in my nature. I do find it interesting that we never received a bill for those times I felt our care was neglectful. I was told I would receive an evaluation form to fill out and return; it never came. Although Greg spent one and a half weeks at the rehab hospital, no medical bill was ever sent to our insurer or to us. I don't know why; I fully expected one. Maybe on some level they knew they had failed us. The doctor I struggled with so much was relieved of his duties some time later. He wasn't a bad man, but for us, he was not a good doctor.

I am so glad that Greg has been able to recover fully from all the physical, emotional, and mental stress his body had to go through. I watch him some days, teasing with his girls, engaging Luke in conversation, or standing at an altar preaching the Word of God, and I can see he is fully back.

Greg's faith is the largest part of his life, and anyone who knows him knows that. Ian Kramer related a story to me that I found remarkable. In the spring of that year Ian was in the gym shooting hoops. When he was finished he went to the locker room to realize he had missed a call. He did not recognize the number on his cell phone, but called it back. The person on the other end of the phone had not meant to call Ian's cell, but thought Ian's name sounded familiar. Ian stated that he played basketball at Marshall. This person asked him if he knew Greg Mirau. Ian said, "Yes, he's my coach." This person told Ian that Greg Mirau had introduced him to Jesus Christ. I tell this story because it reflects so well Greg's life and the impacts. You just never know who knows Greg!

So many wonderful stories; I've only touched the surface of them. On a daily basis I am reminded of the journey God took us through. The clicking of his valve each evening as we crawl in bed is one my daily reminders. I had to work to not resent the noise of it. At first it was a painful reminder of the horrible days in ICU. Now I work to let it be a comfort and reminder of the victory that was achieved.

The leg is a cross to bear. We all wish that the complication would not have occurred. Each morning the leg is stiff and it takes a few steps to get it going. The extra effort to lift the leg when walking without the brace will eventually be a habit. But it will take time. It too is a reminder of our frightening days at the hospital. Simple stretching exercises and sheer will power have allowed Greg to regain much use of his leg. People tell me all the time that if they did not know something was wrong with the leg, they would never be able to tell. We are thankful for each piece of progress.

Scott and Pam Anderson were there from the beginning. Scott said, "It was the nightmare that would not end." Pam stated, "The event became a life of its own." This was a true statement as it consumed almost as much of their lives as it did my own. Their constant loving, caring support went a long ways in helping our family survive.

I wonder sometimes how this life-shaping experience will play out in my kids' lives as they continue to grow and mature. They faced one of the most frightening times of their young lives with a lot of courage. But they held on to faith, hope, and love; surrounded by those who reinforced that for them. They are definitely survivors in a crisis. I pray that God will never let them forget all they gained, and that the fear and pain will fade and the joy of having Dad around will grow.

For myself, I have learned daily to thank God for sparing my husband, for allowing us to continue as a complete family. Many people choose to leave their families, but I wondered going through this how many would still make that choice if faced with our journey. We all know it is important to embrace the moments. I am learning to embrace the small victories. I don't know what tomorrow might bring, but I do know more about how to handle it, where to find strength and support and how to face my fears better.

CHAPTER THIRTY-FIVE

END ON A WIN

"Do you not know that those who run in a race all run, but only one receives the prize? Run in such a way that you may win."
I Corinthians 9:24 NASB

One of the quotes Greg gave to Rick Weegman when he wrote the article for the paper that year was this, "The one thing that I've asked the kids for is for them to end the season with a win, that would be a wonderful thing." When I was reflecting with team members about their year that statement was brought back to me. Dan B. said, "Mrs. Mirau, title the book, End on a Win. It's what Coach Mirau always asked us to do, no matter how we were playing, or what was happening with the team." He went on to say, "It's what Coach did with his battle and life."

I appreciated Dan's insight. I asked many people I interviewed what they would title the book; many of my chapter titles came from their suggestions. Most people when they thought about titles for me reflected their own impacts. One student thought it should be The Measure of a Man. I think there is already a book by that title. John Parr, now a student at Harvard, told me that through Mr. Mirau's battle and success he learned most importantly what true success is. So many of his peers at Harvard talk about their professional choices, the money they want to make, and the kind of home they want to own. He went on to say that for him observing Mr. Mirau's journey and reflecting on the number of people who were there for him, he now redefines what success is. Success isn't the money you make or the possessions you own, "it is measured by the family that loves you and the community that loves you. True success

229

measured is often lost in this day and age," he said in terms of living, "Mr. Mirau is the richest man I know."

Matt Whitaker reflected similar thoughts for the "Excellence in Education" banquet, bringing Mr. Mirau as his guest that spring. Matt said in his written comments, "In the classroom, on the court, or 35' off the ground (hugging the wall to keep my balance on the ladder), I learned that to manufacture a good product I must put in the time and effort. He encouraged me to spend time in the gym and spend time with my books. By applying these principles I learned to excel, yet not until Mr. Mirau almost lost his life did I begin to understand how to live. Mr. Mirau is the most successful man I know. While he recovered from his surgeries, more than 400 people came to visit and support his family. He had made a difference in each one of those people's lives. That is success – a success that far exceeds money and material possessions. That is the reason I will strive to be like Mr. Mirau for the rest of my life." Amazing thoughts and a wonderful testimony of Greg's impact on Matt.

I was reading through Greg's autograph book the other day and was once again amazed by the touching notes. Everything from "We miss you", "Get well", to moving, intimate thoughts about how Greg had personally touched them. The one I found most humorous came from my ever-present sidekick at the hospital, Dave Parr. He said, "Humor is important to us all. You are a man who is full of humor and practical jokes, BUT THIS WAS NOT FUNNY!"

It wasn't funny, but through the difficult journey we did laugh. We had humor in the waiting room, in our home, at the basketball games, even by Greg's bedside. Laughter is healing, and it has been good for us to laugh together as a family and with friends. It is good to see Greg make people laugh again. We have some new friends in our lives through our Bible Study group at church and they say to us often,

Greg is just so funny! Just another sign that he is back, fully healed.

There are so many stories I didn't tell in this book, simple things that meant a lot. One night I stopped by Teresa's, her friend Lynn was at her house working on a scrapbook. Within a few minutes she had us helping her make decisions about the project. Simple things, but helpful in getting my mind off the trial we were in. Or the night that John and Donna Nordstrom, Kevin's parents, made our family a lovely dinner and served it at Kevin's home. The kids and I had not sat around a supper table together for a long time at that point. It was healthy for us to do that.

Other people came and brought support. So many wonderful friends came and visited. Clyde and Roxy gave us a 1000 minute phone card, a great idea so we could call family from the hospital. Treats of food from dear friends who faithfully prayed for us. Large and small financial gifts from so many that alleviated the pressure of wondering about tomorrow.

That spring the Marshall school faculty brought meals to us each week through the end of the school year. Mary Moline made a "Marshall Quilt" and it was raffled off as a fundraiser for us. So many kindnesses, I could never list them all, but they all helped us through each day. One of the ladies who worked in the hospital office said she had never seen so many phone calls or so much mail come for one person. It is so amazing to recognize the depth of support and love that was there for us.

I had a great visit with Bob Newstrom, the fellow coach and friend who gave Greg a ride down to the hospital. He told me that even while they were at the hospital waiting for answers there was humor and laughter. Apparently the nurse to first draw Greg's blood was new and struggled greatly to find a vein. At one point she said, "Uh, oh" and Greg looked at

Bob and said, "Not a good sign when they say that!" Bob said after she left they both had a good laugh. From the start he noted Greg's positive attitude.

The longer we visited the more I could see the impact on Bob's life. It changed his perspective on coaching and what he wants to bring to the young people he gets to influence. He said he really observed how Greg was open about his faith, and how the team picked up on that and used it to carry them through the rough season. Bob said, "It seemed there was so much sense of us against the world." The early injury of his son Pete, (torn spleen during football season), the injury of Geoff Ujdur, (torn ACL during the holiday tournament) and then Greg's life threatening torn aorta.

Bob told me it was like the team had three seasons that year – the first season, the beginning of the year, everything was clicking, they were winning. By the end of December they faced Geoff's injury. In early January Greg was sick, and that began the low time, the second season. He called it "the valley." They learned what it felt like to be a losing team. Pete was recovered enough to join the team, helping to replace the loss of Geoff. During that time Luke stepped up to the plate and became a critical part of the team. The third season was the time the team really came together. They were "us against adversity" and began to see a lot of success.

Through all the seasons of the team was the steadfast belief and hope that they could survive and that their coach would survive. Greg did. He "ended on a win" the most difficult physical battle of his life. But he also knows because of his strong relationship with God if his life had been taken, he would still "end on a win."

Even though the team lost in their first round of the state playoffs, they too ended their season on a win. They had been challenged to think about what is important. That it isn't really if you win or lose; it is how you play the game. They played a vital role in helping our family and Coach Mirau to win his game of fighting for his life. Because of their prayers and support, they saw the real victory of their beloved coach back on the bench. They had the most successful season of their lives.

Chris Olds said, "I've always enjoyed having Mr. Mirau around whether it be just saying 'hi' in the halls at school or when he would watch us play basketball during lunch. It's great having him around at all of our basketball games. He's very encouraging to all of us. He always comes back to the locker room after our games and congratulates us or gives us hugs if we lost. He had to give up officially being one of our coaches, but to me, he is still Coach Mirau."

"Above the influence on our basketball team," says Geoff Ujdur, "Greg's illness made us all realize how lucky we are to live each day and have the people in our lives. The life lesson learned as a result will never leave me and to learn something of such importance and to avert tragedy at the same time is doubly fortunate."

Almost daily I find times to pause and reflect on this story. Sometimes it is while I watch the present team play basketball or watch my kids enjoying a moment with Dad or while we update someone on Greg's progress. It is always with a grateful heart to God and to the family and friends in our lives. Geoff is right; we are doubly fortunate and blessed!

It is encouraging to hear the stories of Greg's impact on others' lives and to know the depth of support that was there for the children and me. Each story holds a special place in my heart. I thank God for those who came, who rallied around us, who gave to us, and stood steadfast by our side. Your efforts made it possible for us as a family to survive the frightening times and through it all to "end on a win." Thank you.

Epilogue

January 2012

It's been 10 years since that traumatic day in January 2002. In some ways it seems longer ago, and yet I could believe it was yesterday, so much of what happened is still fresh in my mind. The fears, the prayers, the support, the drama, and the love will never be forgotten completely. That is a good thing.

Greg still wears a brace to help with the foot-drop. Somedays bringing a fair amount of pain, somedays there isn't any. As a family, we still hear the clicking of his heart valve, but have learned to embrace that sound. It means all is working well.

I asked God for five years when we were in the hospital, hoping he would be here to see his kids complete high school. We are living proof that God answers prayer "above and beyond what we ask or think". Greg watched all of his kids graduate from high school and from college. He attended the wedding of his son, Luke, to Holly Johnson. They have been married for four years.

This past summer, with tears in their eyes, he escorted his daughter Amanda down the aisle to be wed to Jake Radtke. Their shared father/daughter dance was a moment of magic for the two of them.

He is the guidance for Abbey as she pursues God's leading for her future as a young woman of God. The security of her father as protector still brings her much confidence.

And, he is a loving and faithful husband to me. Together we work hard to pass forward to many in our lives the truth of God's unfailing love and mercy. Greg continues coaching and impacting young people at the Marshall School. Parents still to come to tell me he is their child's favorite teacher. (Some things never change!)

So we are blessed. Many people in this book have gone through major changes in their own lives. We have been a part of loving on them through their own journeys. We are grateful for everyone who helped us through. May this story encourage you to:

Trust in the Lord with all your heart, lean not on your own understanding. In all your ways acknowledge him and he will direct your paths" Proverbs 3:5-6.